The Pocket FLOWER EXPERT

Dr. D. G. Hessayon

First edition: 150,000 copies
Published 2001
by Expert Books
a division of Transworld Publishers

A catalogue record for this book is available from   Library

TRANSWORLD PUBLIS'
61-63 Uxbridge Road, Lor
a division of the Random

 Distributed in
by Sterlin
387 F

CONTENTS

Reproduction by Spot On Digital Imaging Ltd, Perivale, Middx. UB6 7JB
Printed and bound by GGP Media GmbH

ISBN 0 903505 55 X   © D.G. HESSAYON 2001

CHAPTER 1

INTRODUCTION

There is no reason to begin by describing the beauty of flowers — in buying this book you have already demonstrated that you are well aware of their importance in the garden. But for all of us there remains much to learn, and despite the welter these days of T.V. shows, CD-ROMs, the Internet and so on we still turn to books for most of our information.

There are times when we want a leisurely read — a chance to look at pictures of other people's gardens, a detailed description of our favourite plants, a design idea or two, a book for the coffee table. There are many excellent books of this type, but this is not one of them.

The role of this book is quite different and relatively unique — its purpose is to provide on-the-spot instant information on the identification, selection and cultivation of the flowers you are likely to find at the garden centre or in the popular plant catalogues. It is designed to be slipped into the pocket or handbag so that it can be taken around the garden or into the shop.

For many years millions of gardeners have turned to The Flower Expert for information on annuals, perennials, bulbs etc. In this pocket version the basic style has been retained but the information has been boiled down to the essential bare facts. All the popular genera have been retained, of course, and so have many unusual ones, but the rarities listed in only a few catalogues have been omitted.

Here then are the things you need to know as you look around the garden you are visiting or the garden centre where you are shopping. What is it called? When does it flower? How tall will it grow? Will it grow in my garden? Checking on this final point is most important — it is folly to buy a pot-grown perennial or a packet of seeds just because the plant in the pot or the picture on the package appeals to you. It is essential to find out whether it will grow in the soil and situation you can provide.

So welcome to the world of garden flowers laid out on the following pages. You will find tiny alpines and man-sized giants, but all share three features. They can all be grown outdoors during their growing season, they do not have a permanent woody framework and they produce sufficient bloom to provide a significant floral display.

PLANT TYPES

ANNUALS & BIENNIALS

An annual is grown from seed and then flowers and dies all in a single round of the seasons.

A **hardy annual** (HA) can withstand frost and so the seeds may be sown outdoors whenever the soil is suitable in spring or in some cases in the previous autumn. This is not the only way of growing hardy annuals — most people prefer to raise or buy them as bedding plants for setting out in May.

A **half-hardy annual** (HHA) cannot withstand frost and having to wait until the danger has passed before sowing outdoors means that the period of flowering is seriously curtailed. For this reason half-hardy annuals are generally treated as bedding plants — seedlings are raised under glass in spring and then planted out in late May-early June.

A **hardy biennial** (HB) is grown from summer-sown seed, producing stems and leaves in the first season and flowering the next. After flowering it dies. It is used for spring-flowering bedding in borders, beds and containers.

BEDDING PLANTS

A bedding plant is transplanted at the leafy stage to its place in the garden or in a container where it provides a display for a limited period. This definition describes a use and not a type of plant. A Pelargonium kept indoors is a 'flowering house plant' or a 'greenhouse plant' — the same specimen planted outdoors in summer is a 'bedding plant'.

Bedding out has traditionally been the main use for these plants — the standard procedure was to fill the flower bed with annuals planted in lines, circles or geometric blocks, but this formality has declined. Flower beds tend to be much more irregular these days, and many bedding plants are now used to fill pockets in a mixed border or rockery. In addition the boom in container growing has led to an increase in interest in bedding plants.

TENDER PERENNIALS

A tender perennial (HHP) is a half-hardy plant which cannot withstand frost. Because of this lack of hardiness it has to spend winter indoors and then return to the garden once the danger of frost has passed. The way the plants are overwintered varies — Pelargoniums are kept under glass as green plants, Dahlias are stored as tubers and Chrysanthemums as roots. Many gardeners treat Pelargoniums and half-hardy Fuchsias as bedding plants which are dumped in autumn.

BOG PLANTS

A bog plant requires damp humus-rich soil which is never allowed to dry out, but it cannot be expected to survive in permanently waterlogged ground. Some experts prefer the term 'poolside plant' as the usual home for these plants is in the swampy soil around a pond, although many bog plants will grow quite happily in a humus-rich border which is kept watered in dry weather.

ROCKERY PERENNIALS

A rockery perennial is a hardy plant which does not produce woody shoots — the leaves and stems usually die down as winter approaches and new shoots appear in spring, but a few are evergreen. Because of its short height, small leaves etc it is associated with the rock garden but these plants are also used at the front of herbaceous and mixed borders.

BORDER PERENNIALS

A border perennial is a hardy plant which does not produce woody shoots — the leaves and stems generally die as winter arrives and new shoots appear in spring, but a few are evergreen. Because of its height, size of leaf etc it is associated with the herbaceous border rather than the rock garden, but these plants are also widely used in mixed borders. The border perennial is one of the permanent features of the garden, although this description can be deceptive — some last for only a few years.

BULBS

A bulb (more correctly a bulbous plant) produces an under-ground fleshy storage organ which is offered for sale in the dormant state for planting in the garden. Included here are the true bulbs, which consist of fleshy or scale-like leaves, together with corms (flattened and thickened stem bases), tubers (swollen roots and stems) and some rhizomes (fleshy creeping stems).

Some bulbs are left in the ground to flower each year, spreading in some cases to form large clumps. Lifting and dividing is only necessary when overcrowding threatens other plants or is affecting the quality of the display.

The other bulbs are grown in the garden for only part of the year. When flowering is over they are lifted and rested indoors as dormant bulbs until planting time comes round again.

CHAPTER 2

GARDEN FLOWERS A - Z

PLANT TYPE
See pages 4-5 for definitions. More than one type may be listed — the most important one first. 'Bulb' means that the plant is usually sold in this dormant form

SPECIES or VARIETIES
In general the species or varieties you are most likely to find at the garden centre. Where the genus is complex a single example of each popular group may be listed

BACKGROUND
Brief notes on the genus — popularity, plant description, ease of cultivation etc

FLOWER TIME
Flowering period in an average season

GENUS

COMMON NAME

TOP TIPS
One or more hints to ensure success

AQUILEGIA

Columbine

. vulgaris 'Nora Barlow'

Border perennial

Rockery perennial

A. 'McKana Hybrids'

The traditional cottage garden Columbine produces short-spurred white or blue flowers. These days there are also long-spurred ones, doubles and dwarfs for the rockery.

VARIETIES

A. vulgaris 'Nivea' – 60 cm. White. Old-fashioned short-spurred variety.
A. v. 'Nora Barlow' – 60 cm. Pink/white. Double.
A. 'McKana Hybrids' – 90 cm. Bright colours. Large flowers.
A. canadensis – 60 cm. Red/yellow. Long spurs.
A. bertolonii – 15 cm. Blue.

SITE & SOIL
5

PROPAGATION
4

FLOWER TIME
May — June

TOP TIPS
Dead-head faded blooms. Water copiously in dry weather.

PROPAGATION
Look up number 4 on the inside back cover for details. 1/10 would mean use either method 1 or 10

FLOWER COLOUR
'Red/yellow' means that each bloom has red and yellow colouring. 'Red or yellow' would mean there are both red and yellow varieties

SITE & SOIL
Look up number 5 on the inside front cover for details of the sun, soil and drainage needs of the plant

HEIGHT
Anticipated height when grown under average conditions. For climbers and trailers denotes length of stem

ACAENA

New Zealand Burr

Rockery perennial

A. microphylla

Provides a 30-60 cm carpet between plants or over stones. The flowers are nothing special but from August onwards there are seed heads (burrs) which are often showy.

VARIETIES

A. microphylla – 5 cm. Red burrs. Bronzy-green leaves.

A. 'Copper Carpet' – 5 cm. Red burrs. Similar to A. microphylla but less invasive.

A. 'Blue Haze' – 10 cm. Dark red burrs. Grey-blue leaves.

A. buchananii – 2 cm. Yellow-green burrs. Dull green leaves.

SITE & SOIL
3

PROPAGATION
2

FLOWER TIME
July — September

TOP TIPS
Be careful to keep it in check if small plants are growing nearby.

ACANTHUS

A. spinosus

Bear's Breeches

Border perennial

A handsome plant grown for its foliage and flower display. The arching leaves are deeply divided and the tubular blooms are borne on tall spires. Good drought tolerance.

VARIETIES

A. spinosus – 1.2 m. White-tipped mauve. This is the one to choose. Large, spiny leaves — take care. Good ground cover, but can be invasive.

A. mollis – 1.5 m. White-tipped mauve. Soft spines, but the leaves and flowers are less attractive than A. spinosus.

A. spinosus

SITE & SOIL
6

PROPAGATION
3

FLOWER TIME
July — September

TOP TIPS
Hates root disturbance — do not lift unless necessary. Buy small plants.

ACHILLEA

A. filipendulina 'Gold Plate'

Yarrow

Border perennial
Rockery perennial

Simple to recognise — flat plates of tiny flowers (usually yellow) above ferny foliage. Good for cutting and drying. Easy and not fussy about soil type. Stake tall varieties.

VARIETIES

A. filipendulina 'Gold Plate' – 1.2 m. Tall variety. Yellow.

A. 'Coronation Gold' – 80 cm. Yellow.

A. 'Moonshine' – 60 cm. Yellow.

A. 'Cerise Queen' – 60 cm. Crimson.

A. 'Paprika' – 60 cm. Orange.

A. ptarmica 'The Pearl' – 80 cm. White.

A. tomentosa – 10 cm. Yellow.

A. 'Coronation Gold'

SITE & SOIL
2

PROPAGATION
4

FLOWER TIME
June — September

TOP TIPS
Hates poorly-drained soil and needs a sunny site. Cut back in autumn.

ACONITUM

A. carmichaelii 'Arendsii'
Monkshood

Border perennial

Once a favourite but now no longer popular. Helmet-shaped flowers are borne on tall spikes above deeply-cut leaves. Good for growing under trees.

A. 'Spark's Variety'

SITE & SOIL
5

PROPAGATION
1

VARIETIES

A. 'Spark's Variety' – 1.2 m. Violet.
A. 'Bressingham Spire' – 90 cm. Violet.
A. cammarum 'Bicolor' – 1.2 m. White/violet. Branching stems.
A. 'Ivorine' – 90 cm. Yellow.
A. carmichaelii 'Arendsii' – 1.2 m. Mauve. Autumn flowering.
A. 'Barker's Variety' – 1.2 m. Violet.

FLOWER TIME
July — August

TOP TIPS
Poisonous — wear gloves when handling. Add compost at planting time.

AETHIONEMA

A. grandiflorum
Aethionema

Rockery perennial

Tightly-packed flower-heads cover this shrubby semi-evergreen in summer. The leaves are fleshy and flower colours range from pale pink to deep rose.

A. 'Warley Rose'

SITE & SOIL
7

PROPAGATION
5

VARIETIES

A. 'Warley Rose' – 15 cm. Rose red. This is the most popular variety.
A. 'Warley Ruber' – 15 cm. Deep rose.
A. grandiflorum – 30 cm. Pale pink. Blue-green leaves.
A. armenum – 15 cm. Pale pink.
A. oppositifolium – 5 cm. Lavender-pink. Blue-grey leaves.

FLOWER TIME
May — July

TOP TIPS
Self-seeds readily so can be invasive. Disappoints when site is shady.

AGAPANTHUS

A. 'Headbourne Hybrid'
African Lily

Border perennial

Clusters of trumpet-shaped flowers appear on long stems above the strap-like leaves. Each flower is about 5 cm long and blue is the usual colour.

A. 'Headbourne Hybrid'

SITE & SOIL
9

PROPAGATION
6

VARIETIES

A. 'Headbourne Hybrids' – 75 cm. Blue or white. These are the ones you are most likely to find.
A. 'Bressingham White' – 75 cm. White. The best white Agapanthus.
A. campanulatus – 90 cm. Blue.
A. 'Lilliput' – 40 cm. Dark blue.
A. 'Tinkerbell' – 45 cm. Blue. Silver-striped leaves.

FLOWER TIME
July — September

TOP TIPS
In cold areas cover crowns with peat or straw over winter.

AGERATUM

A. houstonianum 'Tall Blue'

Floss Flower

Bedding plant: half-hardy annual

The small powder-puff flower-heads are a familiar sight in bedding schemes. There are several colours available but blue and mauve remain the popular ones.

A. houstonianum 'Blue Mink'

VARIETIES

A. houstonianum has produced many named varieties:

A. h. 'Blue Mink' – 20 cm. Mid blue. An old favourite.

A. h. 'Blue Danube' – 15 cm. Blue-mauve. Free-flowering.

A. h. 'Pink Powder Puffs' – 15 cm. Pink.

A. h. 'Tall Blue' – 50 cm. Blue.

SITE & SOIL
10

PROPAGATION
7

FLOWER TIME
June — October

TOP TIPS
Remove faded flower-heads to induce a second flush later in the season.

AJUGA

A. reptans 'Burgundy Glow'

Bugle

Border perennial

An easy-to-grow ground cover. Although planted mainly for its ground-hugging foliage some varieties bear decorative flowers on short stalks. White and pink are the usual colours.

A. reptans 'Multicolor'

VARIETIES

A. reptans has produced several bright-leaved varieties:

A. r. 'Burgundy Glow' – 15 cm. Cream-edged red leaves.

A. r. 'Multicolor' – 15 cm. Green/bronze/cream leaves.

For a floral display choose:

A. r. 'Alba' – 15 cm. White.

A. r. 'Pink Elf' – 15 cm. Pink.

SITE & SOIL
10

PROPAGATION
2

FLOWER TIME
April — June

TOP TIPS
Lift and divide every few years — replant rooted sections.

ALCAEA

A. rosea 'Chater's Double'

Hollyhock

Border perennial
•
Bedding plant: hardy annual or hardy biennial

The spires of funnel-shaped flowers are a familiar sight, but after a couple of years rust disease weakens the plant. Double varieties are more popular than single ones.

A. rosea 'Powder Puffs'

VARIETIES

A. rosea has produced varieties in nearly all colours but blue. Stake if necessary.

A. r. 'Chater's Double' – 1.8 m. Various. Peony-like flowers.

A. r. 'Powder Puffs' – 1.2 m. Various. Ruffled flowers.

A. r. 'Majorette' – 75 cm. Various. Annual – grow from seed.

SITE & SOIL
11

PROPAGATION
8

FLOWER TIME
July — September

TOP TIPS
Grow it as an annual or biennial rather than as a perennial.

ALCHEMILLA

Lady's Mantle

Border perennial
•
Rockery perennial

A ground-cover plant with branching sprays of tiny flowers above lobed leaves. Cut the plants down to just above ground level when flowering has finished.

VARIETIES

A. mollis – 45 cm. Yellow-green. Saw-edged pale green leaves. This is the Alchemilla commonly seen in the herbaceous border.

A. mollis

SITE & SOIL
10

PROPAGATION
6

A. conjuncta – 40 cm. Yellow-green.
A. erythropoda – 25 cm. Yellow-green.
A. alpina – 10 cm. Yellow-green. Dwarf variety for the rockery.

FLOWER TIME
June — July

TOP TIPS
Water in dry weather. Self-sown seedlings can be a nuisance.

ALLIUM

A. moly

Flowering Onion

Bulb
•
Border perennial
•
Rockery perennial

Starry flowers are borne in loose clusters or tightly-packed balls on top of upright stalks. Leaves may be wide or narrow. Alliums are bought as bulbs or growing plants.

VARIETIES

A. giganteum – 1.2 m. Mauve. The tallest Allium.

A. albopilosum

SITE & SOIL
2

PROPAGATION
3

A. albopilosum – 60 cm. Silver-lilac. The largest-headed Allium.
A. aflatunense – 75 cm. Pale purple. Ball-headed.
A. moly – 20 cm. Yellow. Loosely packed stars. Popular.
A. ostrowskianum – 15 cm. Pink.

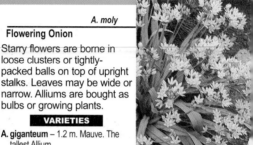

FLOWER TIME
May — July

TOP TIPS
Water copiously in dry weather. Let the leaves die down naturally.

ALYSSUM

A. maritimum 'Little Dorrit'

Bedding Alyssum

Bedding plant:
hardy annual

Dwarf cushions covered with tiny blooms — the traditional partner for Lobelia as an edging around beds. White is the usual colour but there are pink, purple and red ones.

VARIETIES

A. maritimum varieties include:
A. m. 'Snowdrift' – 8 cm. White.
A. m. 'Snow Crystals' – 12 cm. White.

A. maritimum 'Rosie O'Day'

SITE & SOIL
2

PROPAGATION
9

A. m. 'Little Dorrit' – 15 cm. White.
A. m. 'Oriental Night' – 12 cm. Rich purple.
A. m. 'Rosie O'Day' – 12 cm. Dark pink.

FLOWER TIME
June — September

TOP TIPS
Avoid rich soil. Trim off dead blooms and water copiously in dry weather.

✗ALYSSUM

A. montanum
Rockery Alyssum

Rockery perennial

In spring it provides a bright yellow splash and you will see it in rockeries everywhere. The main problem is that it can soon spread and swamp nearby alpines.

VARIETIES

A. saxatile (Gold Dust) is the basic species – 20 cm. Yellow.
A. s. 'Citrinum' – 25 cm. Pale yellow.
A. s. 'Compactum' – 15 cm. Yellow. Neat growth.
A. montanum – 10 cm. Yellow. The best rockery dwarf.
A. spinosum – 40 cm. White. Spine-tipped stems.

A. saxatile

SITE & SOIL
2

PROPAGATION
10

FLOWER TIME
April — June

TOP TIPS
Thrives best in poor soil. Cut back after flowering to keep it in check.

ANAPHALIS

A. yedoensis
Pearl Everlasting

Border perennial

Clumps of grey or silvery leaves spread quite rapidly and in summer large clusters of small starry flowers appear. These white flower-heads can be dried for indoor use.

VARIETIES

A. triplinervis – 45 cm. White. The most popular species.
A. t. 'Summer Snow' – 45 cm. White. Neat growth habit.
A. margaritacea – 50 cm. White. White-edged leaves.
A. yedoensis – 50 cm. White. Leaves woolly below. This species has the largest flower-heads.

A. triplinervis

SITE & SOIL
3

PROPAGATION
2

FLOWER TIME
July — September

TOP TIPS
Easy but it hates dry conditions. Water in times of drought.

ANCHUSA

A. capensis 'Dawn'
Summer Forget-me-not

Bedding plant: hardy annual

Anchusa is usually grown as a perennial, but there is a dwarf annual species which is excellent for bedding and window boxes. Starry blooms cover the branching stems.

VARIETIES

A. capensis is the basic species:
A. c. 'Blue Angel' – 20 cm. Dark blue. The most popular variety.
A. c. 'Blue Bird' – 45 cm. Indigo blue.
A. c. 'Bedding Blue' – 45 cm. Sky blue. Not easy to find.
A. c. 'Dawn' – 20 cm. Mixture of white, pink, blue and mauve.

A. capensis 'Blue Angel'

SITE & SOIL
2

PROPAGATION
9

FLOWER TIME
June — September

TOP TIPS
Cut off flower-heads when first flush has faded. Water in dry weather.

11

ANCHUSA

A. azurea 'Royal Blue'

Alkanet

Border perennial

Few flowers can surpass the vivid blue of Anchusa in the border, but the straggly stems need staking and the plants are short-lived. Mulch around the stems in May.

A. azurea 'Loddon Royalist'

VARIETIES

A. azurea is the only species you are likely to find.

A. a. 'Loddon Royalist' – 90 cm. Blue. The most popular variety.

A. a. 'Royal Blue' – 90 cm. Blue.

A. a. 'Morning Glory' – 1.5 m. White-eyed dark blue.

A. a. 'Dropmore' – 1.5 m. Dark blue.

A. a. 'Little John' – 45 cm. Dark blue.

SITE & SOIL

2

PROPAGATION

6

FLOWER TIME

June — August

TOP TIPS

Dead-head faded blooms. At the end of the season cut down to ground level.

ANEMONE

A. blanda

Anemone

Bulb
•
Border perennial

The bulb varieties are grown from rhizomes or tubers. The Daisy Anemones have narrow petals and the Florist Anemones have poppy-like flowers.

A. coronaria 'de Caen' strain

VARIETIES

A. blanda – 15 cm. Usually blue. The most popular Daisy Anemone. Needs a dry, sunny site.

A. nemorosa – 15 cm. Usually white. Needs a moist, shady site.

A. coronaria – 15-30 cm. Various. Florist Anemones need a sunny site. There are **'de Caen'** (single) and **'St Brigid'** (double) varieties.

SITE & SOIL

12

PROPAGATION

1

FLOWER TIME

March — April

TOP TIPS

Make sure you pick the right type for your site and soil.

ANEMONE

A. hybrida 'September Charm'

Japanese Anemone

Border perennial

Unlike the low-growing bulb Anemones these are tall-growing border plants which produce white or pink 5 cm wide blooms. Cover crowns with peat in winter.

A. hybrida 'Queen Charlotte'

VARIETIES

A. hybrida has several varieties:

A. h. 'September Charm' – 60 cm. Pink.

A. h. 'Queen Charlotte' – 1 m. Pink.

A. h. 'Honorine Jobert' – 1.2 m. White.

A. hupehensis is more compact:

A. h. 'Bressingham Glow' – 45 cm. Rose-red. Semi-double.

SITE & SOIL

4

PROPAGATION

6

FLOWER TIME

August — October

TOP TIPS

Do not remove dead stems until spring. Divide only when necessary.

ANTHEMIS

A. tinctoria 'E.C. Buxton'

Chamomile

Border perennial

A plant for the front or middle of the border. The foliage is finely divided and the daisy-like flowers are borne in large numbers. Each bloom has a central golden boss.

VARIETIES

A. tinctoria – 60 cm. Yellow. This is the Golden Marguerite.

A. t. 'E.C. Buxton' – 60 cm. Cream.

A. t. 'Grallach Gold' – 60 cm. Gold.

A. t. 'Sauce Hollandaise' – 45 cm. Pale cream.

A. t. 'Wargrave' – 45 cm. Yellow.

A. punctata 'Cupaniana' – 30 cm. White. Grey leaves. Not fully hardy.

A. tinctoria 'Grallach Gold'

SITE & SOIL

2

PROPAGATION

2

FLOWER TIME
June — September

TOP TIPS
Staking may be necessary. Cut down the stems after flowering.

ANTIRRHINUM

A. majus 'Magic Carpet'

Snapdragon

Bedding plant: half-hardy annual

The ordinary Snapdragon is known to everyone — 45 cm high with lipped tubular flowers. Nowadays there are variations, including dwarfs and open-faced types.

VARIETIES

A. majus varieties are available in all colours and a range of heights:

A. m. 'Madame Butterfly' – 90 cm. Various.

A. m. 'Coronette' – 55 cm. Various.

A. m. 'Rembrandt' – 45 cm. Red/yellow.

A. m. 'Magic Carpet' – 15 cm. Various.

A. majus 'Rembrandt'

SITE & SOIL

2

PROPAGATION

7

FLOWER TIME
July — October

TOP TIPS
Pinch out tips of seedlings. Dead-head faded spikes.

AQUILEGIA

A. vulgaris 'Nora Barlow'

Columbine

Border perennial
•
Rockery perennial

The traditional cottage garden Columbine produces short-spurred white or blue flowers. These days there are also long-spurred ones, doubles and dwarfs for the rockery.

VARIETIES

A. vulgaris 'Nivea' – 60 cm. White. Old-fashioned short-spurred variety.

A. v. 'Nora Barlow' – 60 cm. Pink/white. Double.

A. 'McKana Hybrids' – 90 cm. Bright colours. Large flowers.

A. canadensis – 60 cm. Red/yellow. Long spurs.

A. bertolonii – 15 cm. Blue.

A. 'McKana Hybrids'

SITE & SOIL

5

PROPAGATION

4

FLOWER TIME
May — June

TOP TIPS
Dead-head faded blooms. Water copiously in dry weather.

13

ARABIS

Rockery perennial

A. albida

SITE & SOIL
3

PROPAGATION
1/10

A. albida 'Flore Pleno'

Rock Cress

A basic component of most rockeries — the grey-leaved carpet is covered with flowers in spring. White is the usual but not the only colour — pink and red are available.

VARIETIES

A. albida – 15 cm. White. The most popular species.
A. a. 'Flore Pleno' – 15 cm. White. Double. Large flowers.
A. a. 'Pink Pearl' – 15 cm. Pink.
A. blepharophylla 'Spring Charm' – 10 cm. Red. Compact growth.
A. ferdinandi-coburgi 'Variegata' – 10 cm. White. Variegated leaves.

FLOWER TIME
March — April

TOP TIPS
Tolerates poor, dry soil. Cut back after flowering to keep the plants in check.

ARCTOTIS

Bedding plant: half-hardy annual

A. hybrida

SITE & SOIL
1

PROPAGATION
7

A. hybrida 'Large-flowered Hybrid Mixture'

African Daisy

You will find the seeds in the catalogues but you may not find the plants at the garden centre. Unfortunately the bright daisy-like flowers close up when the sun goes in.

VARIETIES

A. hybrida – 40 cm. Various. The only ones you are likely to find. 8 cm flowers in white, yellow, blue, orange, red or purple are borne on long branching stems. Stake on exposed sites. Sold as **'Harlequin Mixed'** or **'Large-flowered Hybrid Mixture'**.
A. venusta – 30 cm. Blue.

FLOWER TIME
July — October

TOP TIPS
Pinch out growing tips of 10 cm high seedlings to encourage bushy growth.

ARGYRANTHEMUM

A. frutescens

Bedding plant: tender perennial

A. 'Jamaica Primrose'

SITE & SOIL
2

PROPAGATION
11

Marguerite

A Victorian favourite now coming back as a container plant. May be listed as Chrysanthemum or Anthemis. The daisy-like blooms are about 5 cm across.

VARIETIES

A. frutescens – 80 cm. White petals.
A. 'Chelsea Girl' – 60 cm. White petals. Single.
A. 'Petite Pink' – 30 cm. Pink petals. Single.
A. 'Jamaica Primrose' – 1 m. All-yellow. Single.
A. 'Vancouver' – 90 cm. Pink. Anemone-centred flowers.

FLOWER TIME
July — September

TOP TIPS
Pinch out growing tips to encourage bushy growth. Water in dry weather.

ARMERIA

A. maritima 'Vindictive'

Thrift

Rockery perennial

The grassy leaves are packed into neat mounds and are a common sight in rock gardens and around the seashore. The flower stalks bear globular heads of papery blooms.

VARIETIES

A. maritima – 20 cm. Pink. Several varieties are available:
A. m. 'Alba' – 20 cm. White.
A. m. 'Vindictive' – 15 cm. Pink.
A. m. 'Bloodstone' – 20 cm. Pale red.
A. juniperifolia – 8 cm. Pink. More compact than A. maritima.
A. alliacea – 45 cm. Pink.

A. maritima

SITE & SOIL
2

PROPAGATION
6/10

FLOWER TIME
May — July

TOP TIPS
Do not dig up wild Thrift at the seaside — buy plants at the garden centre.

ARUNCUS

A. dioicus

Goat's Beard

Border perennial

Aruncus is impressive with feathery plumes of tiny cream flowers towering above sprays of pale green leaves. Choose a compact type if space is limited.

VARIETIES

A. dioicus – 1.8 m. Creamy-white. Female plants have greenish-white flowers and decorative seed-heads. Grow at the pool side or back of the border.
A. d. 'Glasnevin' – 1.2 m. Cream.
A. d. 'Kneiffii' – 90 cm. Cream.
A. aethusifolius – 30 cm. Cream. This is the dwarf Aruncus.

A. dioicus

SITE & SOIL
4

PROPAGATION
1

FLOWER TIME
June — July

TOP TIPS
Provide plenty of humus, space and water. Cut the stems down in autumn.

ASPHODELINE

A. albus

Asphodel

Bulb

An easy bulb which should be more popular, but you are only likely to find one species at the garden centre. The tuber-like root is planted 8 cm deep in spring or autumn.

VARIETIES

A. lutea – 1.2 m. Yellow. The only widely available Asphodel. Bright yellow flowers on tall spikes.
A. liburnica – 1 m. Yellow. Slender spikes, late flowering.
A. (Asphodelus) albus – 90 cm. White. Branched flower stems.
A. ramosus – 1 m. White. Similar to A. albus but taller.

A. lutea

SITE & SOIL
2

PROPAGATION
2

FLOWER TIME
May — June

TOP TIPS
Take care not to damage the root when planting. Mulch plants in spring.

ASTER

Border perennial
•
Rockery perennial

A. novi-belgii 'Crimson Brocade'

SITE & SOIL
2

PROPAGATION
2

A. novae-angliae 'September Ruby'

Michaelmas Daisy

True Michaelmas Daisies are the most popular Asters but are not the easiest — powdery mildew may cover the plant. New England Asters have good mildew resistance.

VARIETIES

A. novi-belgii 'Winston S. Churchill' – 75 cm. Ruby. A true Michaelmas Daisy variety.
A. n-b 'Crimson Brocade' – 75 cm. Red.
A. n-b 'Jenny' – 12 cm. Purplish-red.
A. novae-angliae 'September Ruby' – 1.2 m. Dark pink. A New England Aster variety.

FLOWER TIME
September — October

TOP TIPS
Mulch in May, water in dry weather and stake when necessary.

ASTER

Border perennial
•
Rockery perennial

A. thomsonii 'Nanus'

SITE & SOIL
2

PROPAGATION
2

A. alpinus

Aster

In this group of non-Michaelmas Daisy varieties of Aster there are some excellent border and rockery plants which are resistant to powdery mildew.

VARIETIES

A. amellus 'King George' – 60 cm. Violet-blue. September-October.
A. frikartii 'Wonder of Stafa' – 80 cm. Pale lavender. July-October.
A. thomsonii 'Nanus' – 20 cm. Pale blue. July-October.
A. alpinus – 15 cm. Pale purple. May-July. Dwarf Aster for rockeries.
A. a. 'Albus' – 15 cm. White.

FLOWER TIME
Depends on species

TOP TIPS
Mulch in May, water in dry weather and stake when necessary.

ASTILBE

Border perennial
•
Rockery perennial

A. 'Bressingham Beauty'

SITE & SOIL
13

PROPAGATION
2

A. 'Deutschland'

Astilbe

A plant for humus-rich soil. Tiny flowers are borne in showy plumes which can be left for autumn decoration. The foliage is deeply cut and often coppery in spring.

VARIETIES

A. chinensis 'Superba' – 90 cm. Mauve. Good for dry conditions.
A. 'Bressingham Beauty' – 90 cm. Pink.
A. 'Ostrich Plume' – 90 cm. Pink. Arching flower-heads.
A. 'Deutschland' – 60 cm. White.
A. 'Fanal' – 45 cm. Dark red.
A. 'Bronze Elegance' – 25 cm. Pink.

FLOWER TIME
July — August

TOP TIPS
Dig organic matter into the soil before planting. Water in dry weather.

ASTRANTIA

A. maxima
Masterwort

Border perennial

A. major

An easy-to-grow cottage garden plant which will provide pastel shades in the border. Wiry stems bear 2.5 cm wide papery flower-heads — the leaves are deeply divided.

VARIETIES

A. major – 60 cm. Pinkish-green. Varieties are more colourful:
A. m. 'Sunningdale Variegated' – 60 cm. Pinkish-green. Cream- and yellow-splashed leaves.
A. m. 'Rubra' – 60 cm. Wine red.
A. m. 'Rosa' – 60 cm. Pink.
A. m. 'Shaggy' – 60 cm. White.
A. maxima – 60 cm. Pink.

SITE & SOIL
10

PROPAGATION
2

FLOWER TIME
June — July

TOP TIPS
Keep watch for slugs and water in dry weather. Stake if site is exposed.

AUBRIETA

A. 'Doctor Mules'
Aubretia

Rockery perennial

A. deltoidea

The most widely grown of all rock garden plants. The grey-green downy leaves are covered with masses of flowers in spring. An easy plant, but it can be invasive.

VARIETIES

A. deltoidea – 10 cm. Various. This species has produced many garden hybrids:
A. 'Doctor Mules' – 10 cm. Purple.
A. 'Red Carpet' – 10 cm. Red.
A. 'Aureovariegata' – 10 cm. Mauve. Gold-edged leaves.
A. 'Bressingham Pink' – 10 cm. Pink. Double.

SITE & SOIL
14

PROPAGATION
1/10

FLOWER TIME
March — May

TOP TIPS
Cut back after flowering to keep in check and to induce a second flush.

BACOPA

B. 'Snowflake'
Bacopa

Bedding plant: tender perennial

B. 'Snowflake'

A semi-trailing bedding plant which arrived in the 1990s — the pendent stems bear small flowers. It is used in hanging baskets as a foil for brightly-coloured blooms.

VARIETIES

B. 'Snowflake' – 30 cm. White. The stems spread widely to 45 cm, producing large numbers of starry 5-petalled flowers. In spring it is sold by garden centres as rooted cuttings — packets of seed are not available.
B. 'Pink Domino' – 30 cm. Pale pink. Hard to find.

SITE & SOIL
4

PROPAGATION
12

FLOWER TIME
June — October

TOP TIPS
Lift and move the plants indoors before the frosts arrive.

BAPTISIA

B. australis

False Indigo

Border perennial

B. australis

A fine plant for the middle or back of the border — tall spikes of pea-like flowers in summer above attractive clover-like foliage. Can be dried for indoors.

VARIETIES

B. australis – 1.2 m. Indigo blue. The only Baptisia you are likely to find at the garden centre. The 2.5 cm long flowers have orange stamens.

B. lactea – 1.2 m. Purple-flecked white.

B. tinctoria – 1.2 m. Yellow. Not easy to find.

SITE & SOIL
2

PROPAGATION
13

FLOWER TIME
June — August

TOP TIPS
Add compost to the soil before planting. Staking may be necessary.

BEGONIA

B. 'Olympia Starlet'

Fibrous-rooted (Bedding) Begonia

Bedding plant: half-hardy annual

B. semperflorens

Thrives where most annuals fail — in beds which are in shade for much of the day. The fleshy leaves are rounded — colours range from pale green to chocolate brown.

VARIETIES

B. semperflorens – Hybrids are available in white, pink or red.

B. 'Olympia' series – 20 cm. Various.

B. 'Cocktail' series – 15 cm. Various. Brown leaves.

B. 'Devon Gems' series – 15 cm. Various. Brown leaves.

B. 'Coco' series – 10 cm. Various.

SITE & SOIL
15

PROPAGATION
14

FLOWER TIME
June — October

TOP TIPS
Enrich the soil with organic matter and plant in early June (not May).

BEGONIA

B. tuberhybrida 'Fairy Light'

Tuberous-rooted Begonia

Bulb

B. multiflora

Flower size ranges from 15 cm to just 2 cm. All colours from white to near black are available. The fleshy leaves are saw-edged. Water thoroughly in dry weather.

VARIETIES

B. tuberhybrida – 20-45 cm. Various. Large-flowered.

B. t. 'Guardsman' – 30 cm. Red.

B. t. 'Fairy Light' – Red-edged white.

B. multiflora – 20 cm. Various. Small-flowered — **'Non-stop'** and **'Pin-up'** are popular types.

B. pendula – 30-60 cm. Various. Slender drooping stems.

SITE & SOIL
15

PROPAGATION
15

FLOWER TIME
June — September

TOP TIPS
Enrich the soil with compost and plant out in early June (not May).

BELLIS

Bedding plant: hardy biennial

B. perennis

SITE & SOIL
10

PROPAGATION
1/16

B. perennis 'Habanera Blush'

Daisy

The well-known lawn weed has given rise to many garden varieties. Nearly all are doubles without a central disc. All are perennials but are usually grown as biennials.

VARIETIES

B. perennis – 15 cm. Various. This is the basic species.
B. p. 'Monstrosa' – 15 cm. Various. Very large flowers.
B. p. 'Lilliput' – 8 cm. Red.
B. p. 'Pomponette' series – 8 cm. Various. Pompon-like flowers.
B. p. 'Habanera Blush' – 20 cm. Red-tipped white. Quilled petals.

FLOWER TIME
April — July

TOP TIPS
Dead-head regularly if self-sown seedlings would be a problem.

BERGENIA

Border perennial

B. cordifolia

SITE & SOIL
10

PROPAGATION
3

B. 'Silberlicht'

Elephant's Ear

This ground cover thrives under trees, spreads rapidly, effectively keeps down weeds and provides leaf colour all year round. Hyacinth-like flowers appear in spring.

VARIETIES

B. cordifolia – 40 cm. Pink. Drooping flower-heads. It is better to grow one of the named hybrids:
B. 'Sunningdale' – 30 cm. Rose-pink. Red stems.
B. 'Baby Doll' – 30 cm. Pink. Small leaves.
B. 'Silberlicht' – 30 cm. White.
B. 'Evening Glow' – 30 cm. Red.

FLOWER TIME
March — April

TOP TIPS
Cut down when flowering has finished. Remove dead leaves in spring.

BIDENS

Bedding plant: half-hardy annual

B. ferulifolia 'Golden Goddess'

SITE & SOIL
3

PROPAGATION
7/12

B. ferulifolia 'Golden Goddess'

Bidens

One of the new generation of bedding plants introduced in the 1990s. The ferny-leaved stems are studded with large flowers in summer and autumn.

VARIETIES

B. ferulifolia 'Golden Goddess' – 50 cm. Yellow. The long spreading stems can be used for tubs, hanging baskets or as ground cover. Flowers are 4 cm wide.
B. aurea 'Sunshine' – 50 cm. Yellow. A better choice for hanging baskets as stems are pendent rather than spreading.

FLOWER TIME
July — October

TOP TIPS
Overwinter plants under glass and take cuttings in the spring.

BRACHYCOME

B. iberidifolia
'Purple Splendour'

Swan River Daisy

Bedding plant: half-hardy annual

B. iberidifolia

You will find the seeds in the catalogues but you will not often see the plants for sale. Fragrant daisies are borne above the feathery foliage. Good drought resistance.

VARIETIES

B. iberidifolia – 30-60 cm. White, pink, lilac, purple or blue. Flowers 4 cm wide with a black or yellow central disc. Usually sold as a mixture of colours, but named single-colour varieties are available as seeds. The ones to look for are **'Blue Star'**, **'Purple Splendour'** and **'White Splendour'**.

SITE & SOIL
9

PROPAGATION
7

FLOWER TIME
June — September

TOP TIPS
Good soil and protection from strong winds are necessary.

BROWALLIA

B. speciosa
'White Troll'

Bush Violet

Bedding plant: half-hardy annual

B. speciosa

This bushy, weak-stemmed plant has been sold for many years as a house plant — now it has moved out into the garden as an attractive trailer for hanging baskets.

VARIETIES

B. speciosa – 30-45 cm. White-throated violet. This is the species usually offered for sale. There are some attractive varieties listed in the seed catalogues:

B. s. 'Blue Troll' – 25 cm. Blue.
B. s. 'White Troll' – 25 cm. White.
B. s. 'Jingle Bells' – 60 cm. White, blue and lavender mixture.

SITE & SOIL
11

PROPAGATION
7

FLOWER TIME
June — September

TOP TIPS
Choose a sheltered site — not suitable for exposed cold gardens.

BRUNNERA

B. macrophylla
'Variegata'

Perennial Forget-me-not

Border perennial

B. macrophylla

Use it to provide ground cover under trees or for an early floral display at the front of the border. Sprays of starry flowers grow above large heart-shaped leaves.

VARIETIES

B. macrophylla – 45 cm. Pale blue. This is the only species — there are several varieties:
B. m. 'Variegata' – 45 cm. Blue. White-edged leaves.
B. m. 'Hadspen Cream' – 45 cm. Blue. Cream-edged leaves.
B. m. 'Aluminium Spot' – 45 cm. Blue. Silver-spotted leaves.

SITE & SOIL
5

PROPAGATION
2

FLOWER TIME
April — June

TOP TIPS
Water thoroughly in dry weather. Cut down stems after flowering.

CALCEOLARIA

C. rugosa 'Sunshine'
Slipper Flower

Bedding plant:
half-hardy annual

Once a favourite but no longer popular — the French Marigold has taken over the yellow spot. Propagation is a problem — raising plants from seed is difficult.

C. rugosa

SITE & SOIL
10

PROPAGATION
7

VARIETIES

C. rugosa – 30 cm. This is the basic species — it is usual to grow one of the varieties:

C. r. 'Sunshine' – 30 cm. Yellow. The most popular variety. Masses of 2 cm long pouched flowers.

C. r. 'Midas' – 30 cm. Yellow. Earlier than C.r. 'Sunshine'.

C. r. 'Sunset' – 30 cm. Yellow/red.

FLOWER TIME
June — October

TOP TIPS
Choose an F₁ hybrid such as 'Sunshine' if starting from seed.

CALENDULA

C. officinalis 'Fiesta Gitana'
Pot Marigold

Bedding plant:
hardy annual

It may be old-fashioned but it will flourish in sun or partial shade and does not mind poor soil. Easy to grow, but both mildew and greenfly can be problems.

C. officinalis 'Orange King'

SITE & SOIL
10

PROPAGATION
9

VARIETIES

C. officinalis has produced numerous species:

C. o. 'Art Shades' – 60 cm. Various.

C. o. 'Orange King' – 45 cm. Orange. Large flowers.

C. o. 'Lemon Queen' – 45 cm. Yellow.

C. o. 'Fiesta Gitana' – 30 cm. Various. Popular dwarf variety.

FLOWER TIME
May — September

TOP TIPS
Pinch out tips of young stems. Dead-head faded blooms.

CALLISTEPHUS

C. chinensis 'Milady Rose'
China Aster

Bedding plant:
half-hardy annual

You will find a large selection of these chrysanthemum-like plants in the seed catalogues — dwarf and tall, single and double with colours from white to near black.

C. chinensis 'Ostrich Plume'

SITE & SOIL
2

PROPAGATION
9

VARIETIES

C. chinensis is the basic species:

C. c. 'Roundabout' – 20 cm. Various.

C. c. 'Milady' – 30 cm. Various. Ball-like flowers.

C. c. 'Ostrich Plume' – 45 cm. Various. Plume-like flowers.

C. c. 'Matsumoto' – 75 cm. Various. Most popular tall variety.

FLOWER TIME
July — October

TOP TIPS
Mulch in spring, dead-head regularly and stake tall varieties.

CALTHA

Border perennial
• Bog plant

C. palustris
'Flore Pleno'

SITE & SOIL
16

PROPAGATION
17

C. palustris
Marsh Marigold

Caltha cannot tolerate dry soil conditions and so needs a damp border or the boggy ground around a pond. In spring buttercup-like flowers appear on branching stems.

VARIETIES

C. palustris – 30 cm. Yellow. 3-5 cm wide flowers. Single.

C. p. 'Flore Pleno' – 25 cm. Yellow. Double. Masses of flowers.

C. p. 'Alba' – 30 cm. White. Single. Early flowering (March-May) before leaves.

C. laeta – 60 cm. Yellow. 8 cm wide flowers. Single.

FLOWER TIME
April — June

TOP TIPS
Wait until the weather is warm before lifting and dividing clumps.

CAMPANULA

Rockery perennial

C. carpatica

SITE & SOIL
3

PROPAGATION
6/10

C. poscharskyana
Rockery Campanula

You will find a number of Rockery Campanulas at the garden centre. The blooms are bell-like or star-shaped and the colours available are white, blue and purple.

VARIETIES

C. carpatica – 25 cm. White or blue bells. Popular.

C. cochlearifolia – 10 cm. White or blue bells.

C. muralis – 10 cm. Purple bells. Spreads rapidly.

C. poscharskyana – 10 cm. Lavender stars. Spreads rapidly.

C. garganica – 5 cm. White or blue.

FLOWER TIME
June — September

TOP TIPS
Watch out for slugs in spring. Water when the weather is dry.

CAMPANULA

Bedding plant:
hardy biennial

C. medium
'Calycanthema'

SITE & SOIL
3

PROPAGATION
16

C. pyramidalis
Bedding Campanula

The plants in this group are normally grown as biennials and the most popular one is the Canterbury Bell. In early summer numerous spikes of bell-shaped flowers appear.

VARIETIES

C. medium – The Canterbury Bell.

C. m. 'Calycanthema' – 75 cm. Various. The old favourite Cup and Saucer with semi-double flowers.

C. m. 'Bells of Holland' – 45 cm. Various. Single.

C. m. 'Flore Pleno' – 75 cm. Various. Double.

C. pyramidalis – 1.8 m. Various.

FLOWER TIME
May — July

TOP TIPS
Watch out for slugs in spring. Dead-head to prolong floral display.

CAMPANULA

C. latifolia 'Alba'
Border Campanula

Border perennial

C. lactifolia

This group of Campanulas contains the ones grown in borders. The large flowers are cup-shaped or star-faced bells and the usual colours are blue and lavender.

VARIETIES

C. persicifolia – 75 cm. White or blue. Cup-shaped flowers. Popular.
C. p. 'Telham Beauty' – 75 cm. Blue.
C. latifia – 1.2 m. White, lavender or blue. Long bell-like flowers.
C. lactifolia – 1.2 m. Blue, pink or lavender. Open bell-like flowers.
C. glomerata – 60 cm. White, lavender or blue. Globular heads.

SITE & SOIL
4

PROPAGATION
2/10

FLOWER TIME
June — August

TOP TIPS
Watch out for slugs in spring. Dead-head to prolong floral display.

CANNA

C. generalis 'Lucifer'
Canna Lily

Bulb

C. generalis

An eye-catching focal point for the centre of a bedding plant display. The bright flowers are up to 10 cm across and the paddle-shaped leaves are often coloured.

VARIETIES

C. generalis is the basic species:
C. g. 'Assault' – 1.2 m. Red. Purple leaves.
C. g. 'Dazzler' – 1.2 m. Red. Bronze leaves.
C. g. 'Verdi' – 90 cm. Orange-marked yellow/purple. Purple leaves.
C. g. 'Lucifer' – 60 cm. Yellow-edged red. Green leaves.

SITE & SOIL
9

PROPAGATION
18

FLOWER TIME
July — October

TOP TIPS
Not for everyone — it needs a sheltered spot in full sun.

CATANANCHE

C. caerulea 'Major'
Cupid's Dart

Border perennial

C. caerulea

Silvery buds on wiry stems open into daisy-like flowers with papery petals. The ends of the petals are blunt and serrated. Good for cutting, but it has a sparse look.

VARIETIES

C. caerulea – 60 cm. Blue cornflower-like flowers. Narrow, grey-green leaves. Stems need twigs for support.
C. c. 'Major' – 70 cm. Blue. Large flowers. The most popular variety.
C. c. 'Alba' – 60 cm. White.
C. c. 'Bicolor' – 60 cm. White-edged blue.

SITE & SOIL
1

PROPAGATION
6

FLOWER TIME
June — September

TOP TIPS
It will thrive in dry soil. Cut back stems when flowering is over.

CELOSIA

Bedding plant:
half-hardy annual

C. plumosa

SITE & SOIL
14

PROPAGATION
19

C. plumosa 'Dwarf Geisha'
Prince Of Wales Feathers

The plumed ones have feathery flower spikes and can be grown outdoors, but the crested ones with velvety cockscombs can only be grown indoors.

VARIETIES

The Plumed Celosias are varieties of **C. plumosa** — 25-90 cm. White, yellow, orange, red or purple.
C. p. 'Flamingo Feather' – 90 cm. Various.
C. p. 'Rondo' – 25 cm. Various.
C. p. 'Dwarf Geisha' – 25 cm. Various.
C. p. 'Kimono' – 25 cm. Various.

FLOWER TIME
July — September

TOP TIPS
Rather tender — it will not thrive if the bed is exposed to cold winds.

CENTAUREA

Bedding plant:
hardy annual

C. cyanus

SITE & SOIL
3

PROPAGATION
9

*C. cyanus
'Polka Dot'*
Cornflower

Cornflowers are easy to grow — if possible sow where they are to flower. Blue is the usual colour but shades from white to maroon are available. The blooms attract butterflies.

VARIETIES

C. cyanus is the usual species:
C. c. 'Blue Diadem' – 75 cm. Blue.
C. c. 'Frosty' – 75 cm. White-edged various.
C. c. 'Florence' – 45 cm. Various.
C. c. 'Polka Dot' – 30 cm. Various.
C. c. 'Jubilee Gem' – 30 cm. Blue.
C. moschata – 45 cm. Various. Sweet Sultan. Fragrant flowers.

FLOWER TIME
June — September

TOP TIPS
Stake the stems of tall varieties — dead-head when flowers have faded.

CENTAUREA

Border perennial

*C. dealbata
'Steenbergii'*

SITE & SOIL
3

PROPAGATION
2

C. montana
Knapweed

The perennial Centaureas all bear thistle-like heads, producing their main flush of blooms in summer with a second flush in autumn. Dead-head faded blooms.

VARIETIES

C. dealbata – 60 cm. Pinkish-purple.
C. d. 'Steenbergii' – 60 cm. White-centred reddish-pink.
C. d. 'John Coutts' – 60 cm. Yellow-centred pink.
C. macrocephala – 1 m. Yellow. Globular heads.
C. montana – 40 cm. Blue. Flowers in May.

FLOWER TIME
June — July

TOP TIPS
Divide plants every 3 years. Cut down stems to ground level in winter.

CENTRANTHUS

C. ruber 'Albus'
Red Valerian

Border perennial

C. ruber 'Coccineus'

A fine cottage garden plant which anyone can grow — it self-seeds very freely as the clumps growing on old walls clearly demonstrate. The plants are short-lived.

VARIETIES

C. ruber – 45 cm. Pink. Small blooms are borne in large clusters. The varieties are taller and generally more satisfactory, but are less easy to find.

C. r. 'Coccineus' ('Atrococcineus') – 60 cm. Bright crimson.

C. r. 'Albus' ('Albiflorus') – 60 cm. White.

SITE & SOIL
2

PROPAGATION
10

FLOWER TIME
June — October

TOP TIPS
Do not plant in badly-drained soil. Cut down in late autumn.

CERASTIUM

C. tomentosum
Snow-in-summer

Rockery perennial

C. tomentosum

This popular plant has few friends among the experts — the silvery-leaved sheets which flower in early summer can quickly spread and choke out nearby delicate plants.

VARIETIES

C. tomentosum – 60 cm or more. White. The ordinary Snow-in-summer — the 2.5 cm wide flowers have notched petals. There is little to beat it for covering a dry bank.

C. t. 'Columnae' – 60 cm or more. White. Low-growing.

C. alpinum – 30 cm. White. Compact, but difficult to grow.

SITE & SOIL
2

PROPAGATION
6

FLOWER TIME
May — July

TOP TIPS
Do not plant close to choice alpines. Cut back after flowering.

CHEIRANTHUS

C. cheiri 'Cloth of Gold'
Wallflower

Bedding plant: hardy biennial

C. cheiri 'Vulcan'

Millions are planted every October — they flower on erect spikes in March or April (Wallflower) or May (Siberian Wallflower). Yellow, orange and red are the basic colours.

VARIETIES

C. cheiri is the Common Wallflower.

C. c. 'Tom Thumb' – 20 cm. Various.

C. c. 'Bedder' – 30 cm. Various.

C. c. 'Cloth of Gold' – 45 cm. Yellow.

C. c. 'Vulcan' – 45 cm. Red.

C. c. 'Ivory White' – 45 cm. Creamy-white.

C. allionii 'Orange Queen' – 30 cm. Deep orange. Siberian Wallflower.

SITE & SOIL
14

PROPAGATION
16

FLOWER TIME
March — May

TOP TIPS
Dig peat into the nursery bed. Pinch out tips of seedlings. Plant firmly.

CHIONODOXA

C. luciliae

Glory of the Snow

Bulb

A popular spring bulb, but not seen everywhere like crocuses. The six-petalled flowers are borne in sprays — with most types there is a prominent white centre.

VARIETIES

C. luciliae – 20 cm. White-centred pale blue. This is the usual species.
C. l. 'Alba' – 20 cm. White.
C. l. 'Pink Giant' – 20 cm. White-centred rose-pink.
C. sardensis – 20 cm. White-eyed blue.
C. gigantea – 25 cm. Gentian blue. Large flowers.

C. sardensis

SITE & SOIL
3

PROPAGATION
20

FLOWER TIME
February — April

TOP TIPS
Plant in large groups and leave them to naturalise in rockery or grassland.

CHRYSANTHEMUM

C. coronarium 'Golden Gem'

Annual Chrysanthemum

Bedding plant: hardy annual

Only three species now remain under 'Chrysanthemum'. For changed ones see Dendranthema, Argyranthemum, Tanacetum and Leucanthemum.

VARIETIES

C. carinatum – 60 cm. Various. Painted Daisy – flowers are boldly zoned around the disc.
C. coronarium 'Golden Gem' – 30 cm. Yellow. Crown Daisy.
C. c. 'Flore Plenum' – 1 m. Yellow. Double.
C. segetum 'Prado' – 45 cm. Black-centred yellow. Corn Marigold.

C. carinatum

SITE & SOIL
14

PROPAGATION
21

FLOWER TIME
June — July

TOP TIPS
An easy plant, but does not like transplanting. Sow seeds in the garden.

CIMICIFUGA

C. racemosa

Bugbane

Border perennial

Plume-like flowering spikes appear in late summer above clumps of deeply divided leaves. This plant needs water-retentive soil and some shade at midday.

VARIETIES

C. simplex – 1.2 m. White.
C. s. 'White Pearl' – 1.2 m. White. Arching stems.
C. s. 'Elstead's Variety' – 1.2 m. White. Purple buds.
C. racemosa – 1.5 m. White.
C. r. 'Purpurea' – 1.8 m. White. Purple foliage. Easier to find than the species.

C. simplex 'White Pearl'

SITE & SOIL
15

PROPAGATION
2

FLOWER TIME
August — September

TOP TIPS
Mulch in May. Stake if necessary and cut down in November.

CLARKIA

C. pulchella 'Filigree'

Clarkia

Bedding plant: hardy annual

C. elegans

Tiny hollyhock-like flowers are borne on upright spikes — you will find white, pinks, reds and mauves. Pinch out the growing tips of seedlings and be careful not to overwater.

VARIETIES

C. elegans is the usual species.
C. e. 'Double Mixed' – 60 cm. Various. Frilly double.
C. e. 'Royal Bouquet' – 80 cm. Various. Frilly double.
C. e. 'Passion for Purple' – 30 cm. Lilac.
C. pulchella 'Filigree' – 30 cm. Various. Semi-double.

SITE & SOIL
2

PROPAGATION
9

FLOWER TIME
July — September

TOP TIPS
Does not like transplanting — if possible sow where it is to grow.

COBAEA

C. scandens 'Alba'

Cup & Saucer Plant

Bedding plant: half-hardy annual

C. scandens

The stems of this annual attach themselves to supports by means of tendrils arising from the leaf stalks. Useful for providing a quick-growing temporary screen.

VARIETIES

C. scandens – 3 m. Violet. This is the only species. The bell-like 8 cm long flowers with prominent curved stamens appear all summer long, but the display is sometimes disappointing.
C. s. 'Alba' – 3 m. Yellowish-green. Not white despite its name and not as popular as its parent.

SITE & SOIL
2

PROPAGATION
7

FLOWER TIME
July — October

TOP TIPS
Avoid heavy soil and harden off properly before planting out.

COLCHICUM

C. 'Waterlily'

Autumn Crocus

Bulb

C. autumnale

Surprisingly this bulb is not related to the true Crocus. Wineglass-shaped blooms appear in autumn, the long tubes at the base extending into the ground.

VARIETIES

C. autumnale – 15 cm. Lilac. 5 cm wide flowers. In spring the untidy leaves appear.
C. a. 'Roseum Plenum' – 15 cm. Pink. Double.
C. speciosum – 20 cm. Pinkish-purple. 15 cm wide flowers.
C. 'Waterlily' – 15 cm. Pink. Double.
C. 'Lilac Wonder' – 15 cm. Lilac.

SITE & SOIL
15

PROPAGATION
17

FLOWER TIME
September — November

TOP TIPS
Replant divided clumps at once — do not let the bulbs dry out.

CONSOLIDA

C. 'Dwarf Hyacinth-flowered'
Larkspur

Bedding plant: hardy annual

A close relative of the stately Delphinium of the herbaceous border. The spikes bear flowers in white, pink, red or blue — there are short and tall varieties.

VARIETIES

C. 'Giant Imperial'

C. ajacis is the main parent of the many hybrids which are available:

C. 'Giant Imperial' – 1 m. Various. An old favourite. Branches freely.

C. 'Giant Hyacinth-flowered' – 1 m. Various.

C. 'Dwarf Hyacinth-flowered' – 45 cm. Various.

C. 'Dwarf Rocket' – 45 cm. Various.

SITE & SOIL
3

PROPAGATION
9

FLOWER TIME
June — August

TOP TIPS
Does not like trans-planting — if possible sow where it is to grow.

CONVALLARIA

C. majalis 'Variegata'
Lily of the Valley

Bulb

Dainty bells on arching flower stems appear at the same time as the lance-shaped leaves — an excellent choice for spring-flowering ground cover in shady areas.

VARIETIES

C. majalis

C. majalis – 25 cm. White. The 0.5 cm long flowers are fragrant.

C. m. 'Fontin's Giant' – 25 cm. White. Large flowers.

C. m. 'Prolificans' – 25 cm. White. Double.

C. m. 'Rosea' – 25 cm. Pink.

C. m. 'Variegata' – 25 cm. White. Gold-striped green leaves.

SITE & SOIL
8

PROPAGATION
1

FLOWER TIME
April — May

TOP TIPS
Replant divided clumps at once. Pull (do not cut) stems for indoor display.

CONVOLVULUS

C. tricolor 'Blue Flash'
Dwarf Morning Glory

Bedding plant: hardy annual

A bushy plant, unlike its close relative the Common Bindweed. Yellow-hearted 5 cm wide trumpets are borne all summer long, but each flower lasts for only a day.

VARIETIES

C. tricolor 'Royal Ensign'

C. tricolor has several varieties:

C. t. 'Royal Ensign' – 30 cm. Blue. The most popular choice.

C. t. 'Red Ensign' – 30 cm. Red.

C. t. 'Blue Flash' – 20 cm. Blue.

C. t. 'Rainbow Flash' – 20 cm. Various.

Ipomoea purpurea is sometimes sold as **C. major**.

SITE & SOIL
2

PROPAGATION
9

FLOWER TIME
July — September

TOP TIPS
Dead-head spent blooms regularly and water in dry weather.

COREOPSIS

C. grandiflora 'Early Sunrise'
Annual Tickseed

Bedding plant: hardy annual

C. tinctoria 'Dwarf Dazzler'

A free-flowering plant bearing large marigold-like flowers on stiff stems. The colour range is limited — there is yellow, red or brown. Not as popular as the Border Tickseed.

VARIETIES

C. tinctoria has several varieties:
C. t. 'Dwarf Dazzler' – 30 cm. Yellow/red bicolour.
C. t. 'Mahogany Midget' – 30 cm. Brown.
C. grandiflora 'Early Sunrise' – 45 cm. Yellow. Semi-double.
C. 'Cutting Gold' – 45 cm. Yellow. Double.

SITE & SOIL
2

PROPAGATION
9

FLOWER TIME
July — September

TOP TIPS
Choose something else if the site is shady or clayey.

COREOPSIS

C. lanceolata 'Goldfink'
Border Tickseed

Border perennial

C. verticillata

Yellow daisy-like flowers are borne freely on slender stems — excellent for cutting. C. verticillata varieties are the popular choice but they are short-lived.

VARIETIES

C. verticillata 'Grandiflora' – 60 cm. Yellow. Large star-shaped flowers.
C. v. 'Moonbeam' – 50 cm. Lemon yellow.
C. v. 'Zagreb' – 30 cm. Yellow.
C. lanceolata 'Goldfink' – 20 cm. Yellow.
C. rosea 'American Dream' – 25 cm. Pink.

SITE & SOIL
3

PROPAGATION
2

FLOWER TIME
July — October

TOP TIPS
Water in dry weather. Cut down to ground level in late autumn.

CORTADERIA

C. selloana 'Sunningdale Silver'
Pampas Grass

Border perennial

C. selloana

The only grass which is grown for its floral display rather than its foliage. The silvery silky plumes are about 45 cm long — female plants produce the best flower-heads.

VARIETIES

C. selloana – 2 m. Silvery-cream. Arching narrow leaves.
C. s. 'Sunningdale Silver' – 3 m. Silvery-white. Largest plumes.
C. s. 'Gold Band' – 2.2 m. Silvery-cream. Yellow-edged leaves.
C. s. 'Silver Stripe' – 2 m. Silvery-white. White-edged leaves.
C. s. 'Pumila' – 1.2 m. Silvery-yellow.

SITE & SOIL
3

PROPAGATION
13

FLOWER TIME
August — October

TOP TIPS
Remove flower stalks and dead foliage in winter and mulch over crowns.

CORYDALIS

Corydalis

C. flexuosa

Rockery perennial

Border perennial

C. lutea

The tubular flowers are spurred at the back and lipped at the front. Colour depends on the species, and cultivation of these species varies from very easy to difficult.

VARIETIES

C. lutea – 30 cm. Yellow. March-May. Very easy. Self-seeds readily and spreads everywhere.
C. flexuosa – 30 cm. Blue. May-June.
C. cashmeriana – 15 cm. Blue. June-July. Difficult.
C. solida 'George Baker' – 25 cm. Rose-pink. May-June.

SITE & SOIL
4

PROPAGATION
6

FLOWER TIME
Depends on species

TOP TIPS
Species vary too much for any general tips — check label before buying.

COSMOS

Cosmea

C. bipinnatus 'Sonata'

Bedding plant: half-hardy annual

C. bipinnatus 'Sensation'

A popular annual which is easy to recognise — single dahlia-like flowers are carried on slender stems above ferny foliage. Thrives best in poor, sandy soil.

VARIETIES

C. bipinnatus – 90 cm. Numerous varieties are available.
C. b. 'Sensation' – 90 cm. Various.
C. b. 'Purity' – 90 cm. White.
C. b. 'Sonata' series – 45 cm. Various. Very free flowering.
C. b. 'Hot Chocolate' – 45 cm. Petals look and smell like chocolate.

SITE & SOIL
2

PROPAGATION
7

FLOWER TIME
July — October

TOP TIPS
Stake tall varieties — dead-head to prolong the flowering season.

CRAMBE

Giant Seakale

C. cordifolia

Border perennial

C. cordifolia

The cloud effect of the massed tiny white flowers is dramatic — it is seen at its best when grown as a focal point against a dark background.

VARIETIES

C. cordifolia – 2 m. White. An impressive plant with 60 cm leaves and spreading to 2 m. Flowers are borne on a tangled mass of stems. Mulch around the base in May.
C. maritima – 90 cm. White. Common Seakale. Use as a substitute for C. cordifolia where space is limited.

SITE & SOIL
9

PROPAGATION
6

FLOWER TIME
June — July

TOP TIPS
Keep watch for slugs and caterpillars. Cut down in autumn.

CROCOSMIA

C. 'Solfaterre'

Montbretia

Border perennial
•
Bulb

C. crocosmiflora

A plant to grow for flower arranging and for colour in the border. Arching stems carry tubular or starry blooms above sword-like leaves. Not all types are fully hardy.

VARIETIES

C. crocosmiflora has produced numerous hybrids:
C. 'Solfaterre' – 60 cm. Yellow. Semi-tender.
C. 'Lucifer' – 1 m. Red. Hardy.
C. 'Emberglow' – 60 cm. Red. Hardy.
C. 'Emily Mackenzie' – 60 cm. Red/orange. Semi-tender.

SITE & SOIL
9

PROPAGATION
20

FLOWER TIME
July — August

TOP TIPS
Leave dead foliage on plants over winter — cover crown with mulch.

CROCUS

C. sieberi

Crocus

Bulb

C. 'Pickwick'

There are 4 groups. The Dutch Hybrids are the most popular varieties.

VARIETIES

Dutch Hybrids – Largest flowers, March-April. **C. 'Pickwick'** (Purple-striped blue).
Chrysanthus Hybrids – Medium-sized, February-March. **C. 'E. A. Bowles'** (Yellow).
Spring-flowering Species – Small, January-February. **C. sieberi** (Gold-throated lilac).
Autumn-flowering Species – Small, September-December. **C. ochroleucus** (Cream).

SITE & SOIL
3

PROPAGATION
1

FLOWER TIME
Depends on variety

TOP TIPS
Plant corms from different groups for a long-lasting display.

CYANARA

C. cardunculus

Cyanara

Border perennial

C. scolymus

Both species are grown in the vegetable garden for their edible flower-head bases, but they are more often seen in the border for their display of leaf and flower.

VARIETIES

C. cardunculus – 1.8 m. Reddish-purple. This is the Cardoon. The deeply-divided leaves are up to 1 m long. The thistle-like heads are surrounded by spiny bracts.
C. scolymus – 1.5 m. Reddish-purple. This is the Globe Artichoke — more popular as a vegetable but less decorative as a flower.

SITE & SOIL
2

PROPAGATION
6/7

FLOWER TIME
July — September

TOP TIPS
Look for seeds among the vegetable packets rather than the flowers.

CYCLAMEN

Cyclamen

Rockery perennial

Cyclamen is generally regarded as a winter-flowering pot plant, but there are small hardy forms with 2-3 cm wide flowers for growing in a shady rockery or under trees.

C. hederifolium

VARIETIES

C. hederifolium – 10 cm. Pink. September-November. Ivy-shaped marbled leaves.
C. coum – 5 cm. White, pink or red. January-March.
C. repandum – 10 cm. Purple. April-May. Twisted petals.
C. purpurescens – 10 cm. Deep pink. July-September.

SITE & SOIL
8

PROPAGATION
16

FLOWER TIME
Depends on species

TOP TIPS
Mark where it grows — leaves of some species disappear in summer.

DAHLIA

Dahlia

Bedding plant: tender perennial
•
Bulb

Dahlias provide colour when so many flowers are past their best. The Border varieties are the stars, ranging in height from 60 cm to over 1.2 m. Their home is the border — for rockeries, containers or bedded-out areas choose the Bedding or Lilliput varieties which are compact with small flowers. Plant rooted cuttings or sprouted tubers in late May or put in unsprouted tubers a month earlier. Cut down the stems when frosts have blackened the leaves — lift, clean and store the tubers in peat until planting time arrives.

D. 'Athalie'

D. 'Yellow Hammer'

D. 'Little John'

D. 'Hamari Gold'

D. 'Border Princess'

VARIETIES

The most popular flower types are Decorative (Double. Broad florets), Cactus (Double. Narrow and rolled florets) and Semi-cactus (Double. Narrow and partly-rolled florets). All colours but true blue are available. Examples of the wide range of heights include:
Tall Border (over 1.2 m) **D. 'Hamari Gold'** – Gold-bronze, Decorative.
Medium Border (90 cm-1.2 m) **D. 'Athalie'** – Pink, Cactus.
Small Border (60-90 cm) **D. 'Border Princess'** – Gold, Cactus.
Bedding (less than 60 cm) **D. 'Yellow Hammer'** – Yellow, Single.
Lilliput (less than 30 cm) **D. 'Little John'** – Yellow, Single.

SITE & SOIL
3

PROPAGATION
22

FLOWER TIME
July — October

TOP TIPS
Pinch out tips of young plants to increase bushiness. Water during dry spells. Mulch around stems. Remove side buds for larger (but fewer) flowers.

DAHLIA

Bedding plant: half-hardy annual

Annual Dahlia

The knee-high Annual Dahlias should not be regarded as poor relations of the showy varieties on page 32. They are as bright and long-lasting as anything in the border.

D. 'Dandy'

VARIETIES

D. **'Coltness Mixture'** – 45 cm. Various. Single.

D. **'Rigoletto'** – 45 cm. Various. Semi-double. Bushy.

D. **'Dandy'** – 60 cm. Various. Collarette flowers.

D. **'Figaro'** – 30 cm. Various.

D. **'Redskin'** – 45 cm. Various. Semi-double. Bronze-green leaves.

SITE & SOIL
2

PROPAGATION
7

FLOWER TIME
July — October

TOP TIPS
Keep watch for slugs. Do not disbud but dead-head old flowers.

DELPHINIUM

Delphinium

Border perennial

A well-grown tall variety in the border is an impressive sight when in full flower, but unfortunately it is not an easy plant to grow really well. You will have to ensure that the soil is fertile and well-drained, and you should plant good-quality stock in April. You will have to control slugs and it may be necessary to keep powdery mildew in check. Do not neglect watering in dry weather and staking will be necessary for tall varieties. Pinch out tips when stems are 30 cm high to induce bushy growth.

Elatum group

Belladonna group

Pacific group

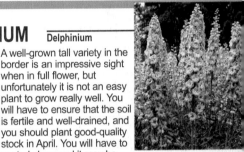

D. 'Lord Butler'

D. 'Pink Sensation'

VARIETIES

There are 3 groups:

The Elatum group has the classical Delphinium shape with large flat flowers crowded on upright spikes. Examples include Tall variety — 1.5-1.8 m. **D. 'Fanfare'** (Blue). Medium variety — 1.2-1.5 m. **D. 'Blue Nile'** (Blue). Dwarf — 90 cm-1.2 m. **D. 'Lord Butler'** (Blue).

The Belladonna group (90 cm-1.2 m) has varieties with slender branching stems and widely-spaced cupped flowers. Examples include **D. 'Pink Sensation'** (Pink).

The Pacific group (1.5 m) consists of Elatum-like varieties which are grown from seed. Examples include **D. 'King Arthur'** (Purple).

SITE & SOIL
9

PROPAGATION
6

FLOWER TIME
June — July

TOP TIPS
Cut back the heads when the main flush has faded to induce an autumn display. Lift in spring every few years and use vigorous sections for replanting.

DENDRANTHEMA Chrysanthemum

**Bedding plant:
tender perennial**
•
Border perennial

*Decorative variety
for exhibition*

*Decorative variety
for garden display*

*Small-flowered variety
for garden display*

SITE & SOIL
1

PROPAGATION
23

Nearly all the 'Chrysanthemum' varieties of old are now classified as Dendranthema. The main block are the Florist Chrysanthemums — here are the showiest types. You will have to decide between Decorative types for cut flowers or exhibition and Small-flowered types for general garden display. In both cases you will have to lift and store the rootstocks (stools) over winter. For a trouble-free display you can grow Garden Chrysanthemums which are hardy. Cut down the stems in winter.

VARIETIES

Florist Chrysanthemums have a wide range of colours and shapes: Incurved (e.g **D. 'Evelyn Bush'**), Intermediate (e.g **D. 'White Allouise'**), Reflexed (e.g **D. 'Regalia'**) etc. Consult a specialist catalogue to choose a variety.

Garden Chrysanthemums are much less numerous. There are Korean Hybrids (60-90 cm) such as **D. 'Ruby Mound'** (Double red) and Rubellum Hybrids (90 cm) such as **D. 'Empress of China'** (Double pink). Finally there are the Garden Mums — 45 cm flower-covered leafy mounds such as **D. 'Holly'** (Pompon yellow).

D. 'White Allouise'

D. 'Holly'

FLOWER TIME
September — October

TOP TIPS
Enrich the site with organic matter. Plant out rooted cuttings in late May — do not plant too deeply. Water during dry spells — feed until the buds begin to swell.

DIANTHUS
*D. barbatus
'Scarlet Beauty'*
Sweet William

**Bedding plant:
hardy biennial**

D. barbatus

SITE & SOIL
14

PROPAGATION
16

Sweet William has densely-packed, flattened heads of pink-like flowers which bridge the gap between the spring- and the traditional summer-flowering bedding plants.

VARIETIES

D. barbatus is the basic species:
D. b. 'Single Flowered Mixed' – 50 cm. Various. Popular mixture.
D. b. 'Scarlet Beauty' – 50 cm. Red.
D. b. 'Auricula-eyed Mixed' – 50 cm. Various. Bicolour flowers.
D. b. 'Indian Carpet' – 15 cm. Various.
D. b. 'Roundabout' – Hardy annual.

FLOWER TIME
May — July

TOP TIPS
Plant in groups — can be grown as a short-lived perennial.

D. 'Chabaud'

DIANTHUS
Annual Carnation, Indian Pink

Bedding plant: half-hardy annual

D. chinensis

There are 2 groups which are grown as annuals from seed — Annual Carnations with double flowers and Indian Pinks with shorter stems and single flowers.

VARIETIES

Annual Carnations are hybrids of **D. caryophyllus**:
D. 'Chabaud' – 45 cm. Various. An old favourite.
D. 'Knight Mixed' – 30 cm. Various. Does not need support.
Indian Pinks have **D. chinensis** as a parent:
D. 'Telstar' – 20 cm. Various.

FLOWER TIME
July — October

TOP TIPS
Water regularly in dry weather. Dead-head faded flowers.

DIANTHUS
Border Carnation, Pinks

Border perennial
•
Rockery perennial

Border Carnation

Old-fashioned Pink

Modern Pink

Rockery Pink

Grouped here are the perennial varieties. Florist Carnations with their large double flowers and serrated petals are the showiest, but they are too tender for the garden. Border Carnations are hardy and have large flowers and stout stems — Pinks have smaller flowers and delicate stems, but the dividing line is blurred. Old-fashioned Pinks produce a single flush of flowers — Modern Pinks grow more quickly and have both summer and autumn flushes. Rockery Pinks are smaller than the other varieties.

VARIETIES

Border Carnations are hybrids of **D. caryophyllus** — 60-90 cm. Flowering period July-August. Examples include **D. 'Hannah Louise'** (Yellow/red).
Old-fashioned Pinks are hybrids of **D. plumarius** — 30 cm. Flowering period June. Examples include **D. 'Mrs. Sinkins'** (White).
Modern Pinks are hybrids of **D. allwoodii** — 20-50 cm. Flowering period June-September. Examples include **D. 'Doris'** (Pink) and **D. 'Devon Glow'** (Red).
Rockery Pinks include several species. Examples are **D. alpinus** — 10 cm. (White. June) and **D. caesius** — 20 cm. (Pink. May-July).

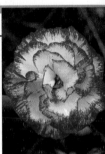
D. 'Hannah Louise'

D. 'Doris'

FLOWER TIME
Depends on variety

TOP TIPS
Replace Border Carnations every few years. Staking is necessary and so is dead-heading to prolong the display. Feed in spring — water in dry weather.

DIASCIA

Diascia

Bedding plant: half-hardy annual
•
Border perennial
•
Rockery perennial

D. 'Pink Queen'

Lax or pendent stems with slender flower spikes appear above a sprawling mat of heart-shaped leaves. Usually grown as an annual, but overwinters in mild regions.

VARIETIES

Varieties for border/rockery:
D. vigilis – 45 cm. Pink.
D. integerrima – 45 cm. Rose.
Varieties for hanging baskets:
D. 'Ruby Field' – 25 cm. Rose.
D. 'Pink Queen' – 25 cm. Pink.
D. 'Lilac Belle' – 20 cm. Mauve.
D. 'Joyce's Choice' – 30 cm. Salmon.

SITE & SOIL
2

PROPAGATION
7

FLOWER TIME
July — October

TOP TIPS
Long flowering period, but stems should be cut back between flushes.

DICENTRA

D. eximia

Bleeding Heart

Border perennial
•
Rockery perennial

D. spectabilis

Arching stems above ferny leaves bear locket-shaped flowers. Choose a sheltered spot as the early leaves can be damaged by cold winds. Suitable for under trees.

VARIETIES

D. spectabilis – 60 cm. Rose-red/white. Tallest and popular but not the best as the leaves die down in summer.
D. eximia – 30 cm. Pink-purple.
D. 'Adrian Bloom' – 30 cm. Red.
D. 'Pearl Drops' – 30 cm. Pink-tinged white.
D. 'Bountiful' – 30 cm. Pink.

SITE & SOIL
5

PROPAGATION
2

FLOWER TIME
May — June

TOP TIPS
Do not hoe close to the stems as roots grow close to the surface.

DICTAMNUS

D. albus

Burning Bush

Border perennial

D. albus 'Purpureus'

A reliable, attractive and unusual perennial. On a warm still day strike a match close to one of the flower-heads and the volatile oils will ignite to produce a blue flame.

VARIETIES

D. albus – 60 cm. White or pale purple. The only species you are likely to find — starry flowers with long stamens are borne on tall spikes. May take several years to establish — do not lift and divide clumps.
D. a. 'Purpureus' – 60 cm. Purple-streaked pink.

SITE & SOIL
17

PROPAGATION
13

FLOWER TIME
June — August

TOP TIPS
Wear gloves when handling — the surface oils are an irritant.

DIERAMA

D. pulcherrimum
Wand Flower

Border perennial
•
Bulb

D. pulcherrimum

Use this one to provide an eye-catching contrast next to a showy perennial in the border. Wiry arching stems bear tubular or bell-shaped flowers above grassy leaves.

VARIETIES

D. pulcherrimum – 1.5 m. Pink or purple. 5 cm long flowers — the only species you are likely to find. Mulch crown in winter.

D. p. 'Album' – 1.5 m. White.

D. p. 'Blackbird' – 1.5 m. Violet.

D. pendulum – 1.5 m. Purple-pink.

D. dracomontanum – 60 cm. Pink. Choose where space is limited.

SITE & SOIL
2

PROPAGATION
6

FLOWER TIME
August — October

TOP TIPS
Buy a pot-grown plant rather than a dormant bulb.

DIGITALIS

D. 'Excelsior'
Foxglove

Bedding plant: hardy biennial
•
Border perennial

D. grandiflora

The tall spikes of flowers will brighten shady borders or woodland areas — not many tall bedding plants can be used in this way. Some perennial species are available.

VARIETIES

D. purpurea – 1.2 m. White, pink or purple. The basic species grown as a biennial — it is better to choose a hybrid:

D. 'Excelsior' – 1.5 m. Various.

D. 'Foxy' – 90 cm. Various. Can be grown as an annual.

D. grandiflora – 60 cm. Yellow. Most popular perennial species.

SITE & SOIL
15

PROPAGATION
16

FLOWER TIME
June — July

TOP TIPS
Foxgloves will not thrive if the site is dry and sunny. Feed in spring.

DIMORPHOTHECA

D. 'Glistening White'
Star of the Veldt

Bedding plant: hardy annual

D. 'Goliath'

Few plants can provide such a sheet of colour in the rockery, but it will only do so if the conditions are right. In a shady spot the flowers will refuse to open.

VARIETIES

D. aurantiaca – 30 cm. Various, around a dark disc. The basic species — choose a hybrid. Good drought tolerance.

D. 'Glistening White' – 30 cm. White. Most popular variety.

D. 'Tetra Polestar' – 40 cm. White.

D. 'Goliath' – 30 cm. Orange.

D. 'Dwarf Salmon' – 20 cm. Orange.

SITE & SOIL
1

PROPAGATION
9

FLOWER TIME
June — September

TOP TIPS
Plant in groups — do not overwater. Dead-head occasionally.

DODECATHEON

D. meadia
Shooting Star

Rockery perennial

The blooms on upright stalks have petals which are swept back to reveal the golden anthers. Eye-catching in early summer but the leaves die down and disappear in winter.

VARIETIES

D. meadia – 45 cm. Rose-purple. The most popular species. Toothed leaves form a basal rosette — watch for slug damage.

D. meadia

SITE & SOIL
15

PROPAGATION
6

D. m. 'Album' – 45 cm. White.
D. pulchellum 'Red Wings' – 20 cm. Pink.
D. dentatum – 20 cm. White. Purple anthers.

FLOWER TIME
May — June

TOP TIPS
Not happy in a typical rockery — needs moist soil and some shade.

DORONICUM

D. orientale 'Spring Beauty'
Leopard's Bane

Border perennial
•
Rockery perennial

There are many yellow daisy-like flowers for the border — pick this one if you want blooms in spring. In many borders Doronicum provides the first splash of colour.

VARIETIES

D. excelsum 'Harpur Crewe' – 90 cm. Yellow. 7 cm wide flowers.

D. excelsum 'Harpur Crewe'

SITE & SOIL
4

PROPAGATION
2

D. 'Miss Mason' – 60 cm. Yellow. 5 cm wide flowers.
D. orientale – 30 cm. Yellow.
D. o. 'Spring Beauty' – 40 cm. Yellow. Double.
D. columnae – 20 cm. Yellow. Dwarf for the rock garden.

FLOWER TIME
April — June

TOP TIPS
Keep watch for slugs. Remove spent blooms to obtain autumn flowers.

ECHINACEA

E. purpurea
Coneflower

Border perennial

The outstanding feature of this late-flowering border perennial is the prominent cone-like disc at the centre of each bloom and the ring of bent-back petals below it.

VARIETIES

E. purpurea – 1.5 m. Purple. Brown cone. This is the popular species. Attractive to bees and butterflies.

E. purpurea 'The King'

SITE & SOIL
2

PROPAGATION
6

E.p. 'Magnus' – 1.5 m. Purple. Orange cone.
E. p. 'The King' – 1.2 m. Pink. Brown cone.
E. p. 'White Swan' – 70 cm. White. Yellow cone.

FLOWER TIME
July — October

TOP TIPS
Dig in compost before planting — feed and water in summer.

ECHINOPS

Globe Thistle

Border perennial

An erect plant for the middle or back of the border. The flower-heads are globular and the stout stems have deeply lobed leaves. Wear gloves when handling.

E. ritro

VARIETIES

SITE & SOIL
2

PROPAGATION
2

E. ritro – 80 cm. Steely blue. The most popular species.
E. r. 'Veitch's Blue' – 1 m. Dark blue. Dark green leaves.
E. r. 'Ruthenicus' – 1 m. Dark blue.
E. bannaticus 'Taplow Blue' – 1.5 m. Pale blue.
E. niveus – 1.5 m. Grey. Green leaves. Grey stems.

FLOWER TIME
July — September

TOP TIPS
Does not do well in shallow soil. Dead-head to prevent self-seeding.

ECHIUM

Annual Borage

Hardy annual

The garden varieties make a welcome change from the usual range of low-growing annuals. The stems branch freely and the upturned bell-like flowers are long-lasting.

E. 'Dwarf Mixed'

VARIETIES

SITE & SOIL
2

PROPAGATION
21

E. plantagineum – 90 cm. Blue. One of the wild species which has given rise to modern garden hybrids — the colour is no longer restricted to blue. Water only when weather is very dry. Staking is not necessary.
E. 'Blue Bedder' – 20 cm. Blue.
E. 'Dwarf Mixed' – 20 cm. White, pink or blue.

FLOWER TIME
June — October

TOP TIPS
Sow where they are to flower rather than raising under glass.

EPILOBIUM

Willowherb

Border perennial
•
Rockery perennial

Heights range from 20 cm to 1.5 m. Flowers are borne singly or in groups. Long seed pods release woolly seeds. Related to the weed Rosebay Willowherb.

E. glabellum

VARIETIES

SITE & SOIL
2

PROPAGATION
2

E. angustifolium 'Album' – 1.5 m. White. The most popular variety. Invasive.
E. fleischeri – 30 cm. Rose-red. Non-invasive.
E. dodonaei – 75 cm. Pink. Invasive — spreads by rhizomes.
E. d. 'Album' – 75 cm. White.
E. glabellum – 20 cm. White.

FLOWER TIME
July — September

TOP TIPS
Buy a non-invasive variety if choice plants are nearby.

EPIMEDIUM

Border perennial

E. grandiflorum

E. versicolor 'Sulphureum'

Bishop's Hat

Epimedium is grown primarily for its ground-covering foliage — leathery leaves which change colour with time. Flowers do appear — pink, yellow, purple or white.

VARIETIES

Some are evergreen:
E. perralchicum 'Frohnleiten' – 10 cm. Yellow.
E. versicolor 'Sulphureum' – 30 cm. Yellow.
E. perralderianum – 25 cm. Yellow.
Others are deciduous:
E. grandiflorum – 25 cm. Various.

SITE & SOIL
5

PROPAGATION
2

FLOWER TIME
April — May

TOP TIPS
Some but not all will tolerate sunny conditions — check before buying.

ERANTHIS

Bulb

E. cilicica

Winter Aconite

Glossy yellow flowers appear in February — each bloom bears a frilly green collar of bracts. The true leaves appear later. Plant the tubers 5 cm deep in September.

VARIETIES

E. hyemalis – 10 cm. Yellow. The most popular species. Early flowering. Self-sown plants can be a nuisance.
E. tubergenii – 10 cm. Yellow. Less invasive, more robust and with larger flowers than E. hyemalis.
E. cilicica – 10 cm. Yellow. Large flowers. Bronze-tinged leaves.

E. hyemalis

SITE & SOIL
3

PROPAGATION
17

FLOWER TIME
February — March

TOP TIPS
Plant the tubers as soon as they arrive. Watch out for self-sown plants.

EREMURUS

Border perennial

E. himalaicus

Foxtail Lily

Tall varieties are used to provide bold upright spikes of tiny starry flowers at the back of the border. A fussy plant which needs deep soil and protection from cold winds.

VARIETIES

E. robustus – 2.4 m. Pale peach. Typical giant species.
E. himalaicus – 1.5 m. White. Easier than most species.
E. bungei – 1.2 m. Yellow. Popular. Like all other species dies down after flowering.
E. 'Shelford Hybrids' – 1.2 m. Various. Easiest to grow.

E. bungei

SITE & SOIL
1

PROPAGATION
2

FLOWER TIME
May — June

TOP TIPS
Plant deeply. Water copiously in dry weather. Cover crowns in autumn.

ERIGERON

E. aureus

Fleabane

Border perennial

Rockery perennial

E. 'Foerster's Liebling'

E. 'Dignity'

Looks like a small Michaelmas Daisy, but the petals are more numerous and it blooms earlier. A useful front-of-the-border plant with yellow-centred flowers.

VARIETIES

E. 'Prosperity' – 40 cm. Pale blue.
E. 'Darkest of All' – 60 cm. Violet.
E. 'Dignity' – 50 cm. Lilac.
E. 'Rosa Juwel' – 60 cm. Pink.
E. 'Foerster's Liebling' – 60 cm. Pink.
E. karvinskianus – 15 cm. White, ageing to purple. Invasive.
E. aureus – 10 cm. Yellow.

SITE & SOIL
2

PROPAGATION
6

FLOWER TIME
June — August

TOP TIPS
Support the stems of tall varieties — cut down to ground level in autumn.

ERODIUM

E. variabile 'Roseum'

Stork's Bill

Rockery perennial

Border perennial

E. corsicum

A geranium-like plant with varieties for the rockery and the border — the foliage is generally attractive. The flowers are usually red-veined white or pink.

VARIETIES

E. manescaui – 45 cm. Magenta. Most popular border variety.
E. variabile 'Roseum' – 8 cm. Pink. Cushion-like growth.
E. v. 'Ken Aslet' – 8 cm. Pink.
E. corsicum – 8 cm. Pink. Silvery leaves. Mat-like growth.
E. chrysanthum – 15 cm. Yellow. Mound-like growth.

SITE & SOIL
2

PROPAGATION
6

FLOWER TIME
June — August

TOP TIPS
A good choice for chalky soil — hardy and long-lived.

ERYNGIUM

E. bourgatii

Sea Holly

Border perennial

E. oliverianum

Easy to recognise — thistle-like leaves form a rosette and thimble-shaped flower-heads with an intricately-spined ruff are borne on branching stems. Flowers last for months.

VARIETIES

E. planum – 80 cm. Pale blue. The most popular variety. Evergreen.
E. variifolium – 60 cm. Grey-blue. White-veined leaves. Evergreen.
E. oliverianum – 80 cm. Steely blue.
E. bourgatii – 60 cm. Blue. Attractive leaves.
E. paniculatum – 1.2 m. Pale green.
E. alpinum – 60 cm. Blue.

SITE & SOIL
14

PROPAGATION
6

FLOWER TIME
July — September

TOP TIPS
Cut down to ground level in autumn. Dislikes root disturbance.

ERYSIMUM

E. 'Bowles Mauve'
Perennial Wallflower

Border perennial

Rockery perennial

E. 'Orange Flame'

Unlike its better known biennial relative the variety in the photograph stays in bloom for many months. Colours range from pale yellow to dark red. Easy but not long-lived.

VARIETIES

E. 'Bowles Mauve' – 75 cm. Mauve. The most popular variety which blooms nearly all year round. Vigorous and bushy — evergreen.

E. 'Harpur Crewe' – 50 cm. Yellow. April-May.

E. 'Plantworld Gold' – 40 cm. Gold/mauve. April-June.

E. 'Orange Flame' – 30 cm. Gold.

SITE & SOIL
14

PROPAGATION
10

FLOWER TIME
Depends on variety

TOP TIPS
Trim back after flowering to keep the plant bushy. Water in summer.

ERYTHRONIUM

E. 'Pagoda'
Dog's Tooth Violet

Bulb

E. dens-canis

The common name comes from the shape of the tubers and not the flowers. Good for growing under trees — nodding flowers droop at the top of wiry stems.

VARIETIES

E. dens-canis – 15 cm. Pink. Flowers 5 cm across. Brown-blotched leaves. White, pink and violet varieties are available.

E. 'Pagoda' – 25 cm. Yellow.

E. 'Americanum' – 10 cm. Yellow.

E. californicum 'White Beauty' – 30 cm. Red-eyed white. Mottled leaves. The showiest Erythronium.

SITE & SOIL
8

PROPAGATION
13

FLOWER TIME
April — May

TOP TIPS
Do not let the tubers dry out before planting. Dislikes root disturbance.

ESCHSCHOLZIA

E. 'Single Mixed'
Californian Poppy

Hardy annual

E. californica

Few plants are easier to raise — a sprinkling of seed in spring over bare ground produces a summer-long show of silky-petalled flowers. Does not do well in rich soil.

VARIETIES

E. californica – 30 cm. Various. This species is the parent of many hybrids:

E. 'Single Mixed' – 30 cm. Various.

E. 'Art Shades' – 30 cm. Various. Semi-double. Frilled petals.

E. 'Prima Ballerina' – 30 cm. Various. Double. Fluted petals.

E. 'Dalli' – 30 cm. Red/yellow.

SITE & SOIL
1

PROPAGATION
21

FLOWER TIME
June — September

TOP TIPS
Do not transplant — sow where it is to flower. Dead-head regularly.

EUPATORIUM

E. purpureum
Eupatorium

Border perennial
•
Bog plant

A plant for a damp semi-wild area or a bog garden. In late summer clusters of tiny fluffy flowers are borne in dense heads on top of tall leafy stems.

E. purpureum

SITE & SOIL
16

PROPAGATION
1

VARIETIES
E. cannabinum – 1.8 m. Reddish-purple. Hemp Agrimony.
E. c. 'Flore Pleno' – 1.8 m. Pink. Double.
E. purpureum – 1.8 m. Reddish-purple. Purple stems.
E. p. 'Atropurpureum' – 1.8 m. Reddish-purple. Purple leaves.
E. rugosum – 1.2 m. White.

FLOWER TIME
August — September

TOP TIPS
Moist soil is essential. Cut down stems after flowering.

EUPHORBIA

E. griffithii
Spurge

Border perennial
•
Rockery perennial

The true flowers are insignificant — the floral display comes from the petal-like bracts. You can pick colourful leaves, bright flower-heads and/or winter foliage.

E. polychroma

SITE & SOIL
4

PROPAGATION
2

VARIETIES
E. polychroma – 45 cm. Yellow.
E. myrsinites – 10 cm. Yellow. Semi-prostrate.
E. characias 'Wulfenii' – 1.5 m. Yellow. Blue-green leaves.
E. griffithii – 80 cm. Orange. Bronzy leaves.
E. amygdaloides 'Robbiae' – 45 cm. Yellow. Good evergreen.

FLOWER TIME
April — May

TOP TIPS
Some varieties are invasive. Handle with care as sap is irritating.

EUSTOMA

E. 'Mermaid Blue'
Prairie Gentian

Bedding plant: half-hardy annual

It was first introduced as a house plant and then as a bedding plant in the 1990s. The 5 cm wide bell-shaped flowers are borne on sturdy stems.

E. russellianum

SITE & SOIL
2

PROPAGATION
25

VARIETIES
E. (Lisianthus) russellianum – 60 cm. Pale purple. The basic species, now replaced by hybrids.
E. 'Heidi' series – 45 cm. Various, including bicolours.
E. 'Yodel' series – 45 cm. Various.
E. 'Echo' series – 45 cm. Various. Double.
E. 'Mermaid Blue' – 15 cm. Violet.

FLOWER TIME
July — September

TOP TIPS
Check that shop-bought seedlings have been properly hardened off.

FELICIA

**Bedding plant:
half-hardy annual**

F. bergeriana

SITE & SOIL
1

PROPAGATION
7

F. amelloides
Kingfisher Daisy

A bright blue South African daisy-like plant which is eye-catching on a sunny day but the petals close up in dull weather. Light land is best — take care not to overwater.

VARIETIES

F. amelloides – 45 cm. Blue. A tall species with several varieties:
F. a. 'Santa Anita' – 45 cm. Blue. Large flowers.
F. a. 'Variegata' – 45 cm. Blue. Cream-edged leaves.
F. heterophylla – 25 cm. Blue. More reliable than F. amelloides.
F. bergeriana – 10 cm. Blue.

FLOWER TIME
July — October

TOP TIPS
Quite tender, so not a good choice for exposed or partly shady sites.

FILIPENDULA

Border perennial
Bog plant

*F. hexapetala
'Plena'*

SITE & SOIL
15

PROPAGATION
2

F. purpurea
Meadowsweet

The stems bear terminal clusters of small flowers. It is quite easy to grow provided the soil is not allowed to dry out and there is some shade during the day.

VARIETIES

F. hexapetala – 75 cm. White or pink-tinged white. Ferny leaves.
F. h. 'Plena' – 75 cm. White or pink-tinged white. Double.
F. h. 'Rosea' – 75 cm. Pink.
F. purpurea – 1.2 m. Rose. Flat flower-heads.
F. rubra 'Venusta' – 1.8 m. Pink. Wide flower-heads.

FLOWER TIME
June — July

TOP TIPS
Add organic matter before planting — moist soil is essential.

FRAGARIA

Border perennial

F. chiloensis

SITE & SOIL
15

PROPAGATION
26

F. 'Pink Panda'
Ornamental Strawberry

A shade-loving ground cover grown for its strawberry-like flowers and fruits — these fruits are for display and not usually for the table. Leaves are made up of three leaflets.

VARIETIES

F. (Duchesnea) indica – 10 cm. Yellow. Indian Strawberry. This is the one you are most likely to find.
F. i. 'Harlequin' – 10 cm. Yellow. Speckled leaves.
F. 'Pink Panda' – 10 cm. Pink.
F. vesca – 30 cm. White.
F. chiloensis – 30 cm. White. Edible red fruit.

FLOWER TIME
May — September

TOP TIPS
Can be invasive — avoid planting close to low-growing neighbours.

FRITILLARIA

F. imperialis 'Maxima Lutea'

Fritillary

Bulb

All the Fritillarias have bell-like blooms which generally hang down from the top of upright stems, but the two popular species are quite different from each other.

F. meleagris

VARIETIES

F. meleagris – 30 cm. Various. Snake's Head Fritillary. 1-2 flowers per stem.
F. m. 'Alba' – 30 cm. White.
F. imperialis – 75 cm. Various. Crown Imperial. Numerous flowers per stem — crown of leaves above.
F. i. 'Maxima Lutea' – 75 cm. Yellow.
F. i. 'Aurora' – 75 cm. Orange.

SITE & SOIL
2

PROPAGATION
3

FLOWER TIME
April — May

TOP TIPS
Handle bulbs carefully when planting and do not let them dry out.

FUCHSIA

Fuchsia

Border perennial
•
Bedding plant: tender perennial
•
Bedding plant: half-hardy annual

F. magellanica 'Riccartonii'

F. 'Mrs. Popple'

F. 'Swingtime'

The usual flower pattern is four swept-back sepals with petals and stamens hanging below, but there are exceptions. There are three major groups. The Border Fuchsias are hardy, producing graceful arching branches year after year — these branches are killed by frost. The Bedding Fuchsias are raised from cuttings or seeds for planting out when the frosts have passed. Finally there are the Trailing Fuchsias which are non-hardy varieties with weak stems for hanging baskets.

F. 'Alice Hoffman'

VARIETIES

There are many Border Fuchsias:
F. magellanica – 1.2 m. Red/purple. The most popular species.
F. m. 'Riccartonii' – 1.2 m. Red/purple. An old favourite.
F. m. 'Alba' – 1.2 m. White/mauve.
F. 'Alice Hoffman' – 50 cm. Red/white.
F. 'Mrs. Popple' – 1 m. Red/purple.
Bedding Fuchsias are more numerous:
F. 'Rufus' – 60 cm. Red.
F. 'Thalia' – 60 cm. Red. Tubular flowers in clusters.
There are fewer Trailing Fuchsias:
F. 'Swingtime' – 50 cm. Red/white.

F. 'Thalia'

SITE & SOIL
13

PROPAGATION
12/25

FLOWER TIME
July — October

TOP TIPS
Pinch back tips of young plants to induce bushiness. Water copiously in dry weather and feed occasionally. Lift and pot up non-hardy types in October.

GAILLARDIA

Border perennial

G. *'Dazzler'*
Blanket Flower

A popular herbaceous border plant — the daisy-like 5-10 cm wide flowers have red, yellow or orange petals which are usually tipped with yellow or orange.

VARIETIES

G. grandiflora – 60 cm. Orange/yellow. Numerous hybrids are available:

G. 'Dazzler' – 75 cm. Red-centred yellow.

G. 'Wirral Flame' – 75 cm. Yellow-edged red.

G. 'Burgunder' – 60 cm. Red.

G. 'Goblin' – 30 cm. Yellow/red.

G. *'Wirral Flame'*

SITE & SOIL
2

PROPAGATION
6

FLOWER TIME
June — September

TOP TIPS
Growth deteriorates with age — divide clumps every 3 years.

GALANTHUS

Bulb

G. *'Atkinsii'*
Snowdrop

Small pendent flowers — the curtain-raiser of the gardening year. You can tell it from Leucojum by the 3 green-tipped petals and 3 outer all-white ones.

VARIETIES

G. nivalis – 15 cm. White. Common Snowdrop.

G. n. 'Flore Pleno' – 15 cm. White. Double.

G. n. 'Ophelia' – 15 cm. White. Double.

G. n. 'Lutescens' – 15 cm. Yellow-marked white.

G. 'Atkinsii' – 25 cm. White. Early.

G. *nivalis*

SITE & SOIL
15

PROPAGATION
20

FLOWER TIME
January — March

TOP TIPS
Plant the bulbs as soon as possible after purchase.

GALEGA

Border perennial

G. *officinalis*
Goat's Rue

An easy plant which will thrive in sun or shade, but its untidy growth habit is more suited to the cottage garden than the herbaceous border. Cut down when flowering has finished.

VARIETIES

G. officinalis – 1.2 m. Mauve. Branched stems. Spikes of pea-like flowers.

G. o. 'Alba' – 1.2 m. White.

G. orientalis – 1.2 m. Violet.

There are several hybrids:

G. 'His Majesty' – 1.5 m. Pink/white.

G. 'Lady Wilson' – 1.5 m. Mauve/cream.

G. *'His Majesty'*

SITE & SOIL
4

PROPAGATION
1

FLOWER TIME
June — September

TOP TIPS
Useful for growing through tall shrubs which provide support.

GALTONIA

Bulb

G. candicans
Summer Hyacinth

An imposing plant for the middle of the border — the tall flower stalks are clothed with 20 or more hanging white bells. The leaves are long and strap-like.

VARIETIES

G. candicans – 90 cm. White. The only popular species — looks like a giant and elongated Hyacinth. Plant the bulbs 15 cm deep in spring. Cut off the stalks when flowers have withered. Dislikes root disturbance.

G. viridiflora – 90 cm. Pale green. Wide leaves.

G. princeps – 60 cm. Pale green.

G. candicans

SITE & SOIL
9

PROPAGATION
13

FLOWER TIME
August — September

TOP TIPS
Protect young leaves from slugs. Cover crowns with mulch in winter.

GAZANIA

Bedding plant: half-hardy annual

G. 'Sundance'
Gazania

Each large daisy-like flower bears petals which arch backwards to reveal the central dark-coloured ring around the disc. Flowers close up in dull weather.

VARIETIES

G. 'Talent Mixed' – 20 cm. Various. Silvery-grey leaves.

G. 'Harlequin' – 40 cm. Various.

G. 'Sundance' – 30 cm. Various. Large flowers.

G. 'Chansonette' – 20 cm. Various.

G. 'Mini-Star' – 20 cm. Various.

G. 'Daybreak Red Stripe' – 25 cm. Yellow/red. Striped flowers.

G. 'Harlequin'

SITE & SOIL
1

PROPAGATION
7

FLOWER TIME
July — October

TOP TIPS
This annual will do badly in heavy or badly-drained soil.

GENTIANA

Rockery perennial

G. septemfida
Gentian

All require free-draining soil, but other likes and dislikes vary with the species. Some like lime and others hate it — some are easy and others are temperamental.

VARIETIES

G. septemfida – 20 cm. Blue-purple. July-August. Easiest to grow.

G. asclepiadea – 75 cm. Blue. July-August.

G. lutea – 1.5 m. Yellow. July.

G. acaulis – 8 cm. Blue. May-June.

G. verna – 6 cm. Blue. May.

G. sino-ornata – 15 cm. Green-striped blue. September-October.

G. acaulis

SITE & SOIL
3

PROPAGATION
6/17

FLOWER TIME
Depends on species

TOP TIPS
Always check soil and site requirements before buying a plant.

GERANIUM

Crane's Bill

Border perennial
•
Rockery perennial

G. psilostemon

G. platypetalum

Geraniums (do not confuse with the showy half-hardy Pelargonium) have few rivals if you are looking for easy-to-grow and drought-tolerant ground cover. The leaves may be green, red, grey or bronze — the flowers are white, pink, red, blue, mauve or violet. Many types lose their leaves in winter but some are evergreen — many varieties will flourish in light or partial shade but some do best in a sunny situation. This means that you should never buy a Geranium without checking its likes and dislikes on the label.

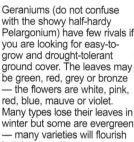

G. oxonianum 'Wargrave Pink'

VARIETIES

Tall varieties (over 60 cm):
   G. psilostemon – Magenta.
Medium varieties (30-60 cm):
   G. oxonianum 'Wargrave Pink' – Salmon-pink. Evergreen.
   G. 'Johnson's Blue' – Blue.
   G. 'Ann Folkard' – Magenta.
Low-growing varieties (15-30 cm):
   G. macrorrhizum 'Ingwersen's Variety' – Pink. Evergreen.
   G. wallichianum 'Buxton's Variety' – Blue. Evergreen.
   G. platypetalum – Violet-blue.
Dwarf varieties (less than 15 cm):
   G. cinereum 'Ballerina' – Dark-veined pink. Evergreen.
   G. sanguineum 'Striatum' – Dark-veined pink.

G. cinereum 'Ballerina'

SITE & SOIL
12

PROPAGATION
2

G. sanguineum 'Striatum'

FLOWER TIME
July — September

TOP TIPS
If the ground is poor dig in well-rotted manure or garden compost before planting. Feed around the stems in spring. Cut back in late summer if growth has become untidy.

GEUM

Avens

Border perennial
•
Rockery perennial
•
Bog plant

G. 'Lady Stratheden'

G. 'Mrs. J. Bradshaw'

The popular varieties form dense clumps at the front of the border — in early summer the bright, bowl-shaped flowers appear. There are also a few dwarf types.

VARIETIES

G. chiloense (45 cm) is the basic species. Hybrids include:
G. 'Mrs. J. Bradshaw' – Scarlet.
G. 'Lady Stratheden' – Yellow.
G. 'Borisii' – Orange.
G. montanum – 15 cm. Yellow. The most popular rockery Geum.
G. rivale – 45 cm. Pink bells. The most popular bog-garden Geum.

SITE & SOIL
3

PROPAGATION
2

FLOWER TIME
May — August

TOP TIPS
Add organic matter to the soil before planting. Divide every few years.

GLADIOLUS
Sword Lily

Bulb

G. 'Flower Song'

G. 'Columbine'

G. 'Melodie'

G. 'Greenbird'

SITE & SOIL
2

PROPAGATION
27

The sword-like leaves and one-sided flower spikes are known to everyone, but the differences between the various types are surprisingly large. Heights range from 30 cm to 1.2 m and flowers may be as small as an egg cup or as wide as a saucer. Petal edges are plain or frilled and a few species are hardy. By far the most popular group are the Large-flowered Hybrids — plant the corms in spring and lift in October. Store the soil-free corms in a cool and dry place until spring. Staking is usually necessary.

G. 'Peter Pears'

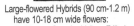
VARIETIES

Large-flowered Hybrids (90 cm-1.2 m) have 10-18 cm wide flowers:
  G. 'Flower Song' – Yellow. Frilled.
  G. 'Peter Pears' – Red/salmon.
Primulinus Hybrids (45-90 cm) have 8 cm wide hooded flowers loosely arranged on the stems:
  G. 'Columbine' – Pink/white.
Butterfly Hybrids (60 cm-1.2 m) have 10 cm wide brightly-throated flowers closely arranged on the stems:
  G. 'Melodie' – Red-throated pink.
Miniature Hybrids (45-60 cm) have 5 cm wide primulinus-like flowers:
  G. 'Greenbird' – Yellowish-green.
Species Gladioli flower in early summer:
  G. byzantinus – Magenta. Hardy.

G. byzantinus

FLOWER TIME
July — September

TOP TIPS
Water thoroughly during dry weather once the flower spikes have appeared. Plant the corms 10 cm deep in March-May (hybrids) or October (hardy species).

GODETIA
Godetia

G. 'Salmon Princess'

Hardy annual

G. 'Sybil Sherwood'

SITE & SOIL
2

PROPAGATION
21

Large flowers with fluted papery petals are borne freely on upright leafy spikes — the flowering season is quite short. If possible sow seeds where the plants are to grow.

VARIETIES

G. grandiflora hybrids:
G. 'Grace Mixed' – 60 cm. Various.
G. 'Sybil Sherwood' – 40 cm. White-edged pink.
G. 'Azalea-flowered Mixed' – 40 cm. Various. Semi-double.
G. 'Salmon Princess' – 20 cm. Salmon.
G. 'Dwarf Satin' – 20 cm. Various.

FLOWER TIME
July — September

TOP TIPS
Water when the weather is dry. Stake tall varieties. Do not overfeed.

GOMPHRENA

G. globosa
Globe Amaranth

Bedding plant: half-hardy annual

G. 'Strawberry Fields'

You will not find Gomphrena in the bedding plant section of your garden centre but you will find the seeds in the larger catalogues. Good for cutting and drying.

VARIETIES

G. globosa is the basic species. There are several hybrids with ball-like flowers on stiff stems:
G. 'Strawberry Fields' – 80 cm. Red.
G. 'Chuckles' – 60 cm. Various.
G. 'Pink Pinheads' – 45 cm. Dark pink. Trailing stems.
G. 'Buddy' – 15 cm. Purple.

SITE & SOIL
2

PROPAGATION
7

FLOWER TIME
July — October

TOP TIPS
Trouble-free, but benefits from occasional feeding in summer.

GYPSOPHILA

G. repens 'Dorothy Teacher'
Perennial Baby's Breath

Border perennial
Rockery perennial

G. paniculata 'Bristol Fairy'

A welcome relief from the large-flowered plants in the border — a billowy cloud of tiny white or pink flowers appear on thin stems above grey-green grassy leaves.

VARIETIES

G. paniculata is the border species:
G. p. 'Bristol Fairy' – 90 cm. White. Double. The usual choice.
G. p. 'Flamingo' – 90 cm. Pink. Double.
G. repens is the rockery species:
G. r. 'Dorothy Teacher' – 15 cm. Pink. Double.
G. r. 'Dubia' – 15 cm. White. Single.

SITE & SOIL
14

PROPAGATION
10

FLOWER TIME
July — August

TOP TIPS
Do not lift and divide plants. Cut down in autumn.

GYPSOPHILA

G. elegans 'Covent Garden'
Annual Baby's Breath

Bedding plant: hardy annual

G. elegans

Provides sprays of tiny flowers for beds and flower arrangers. The flowering period is short, so successional planting is necessary to provide a July to October display.

VARIETIES

G. elegans is the usual species – there are several varieties:
G. e. 'Covent Garden' – 45 cm. White.
G. e. 'Monarch' – 30 cm. White.
G. e. 'Bright Rose' – 45 cm. Pink.
G. muralis 'Garden Bride' – 20 cm. Pink. Single.
G. m. 'Gypsy' – 20 cm. Pink. Double.

SITE & SOIL
14

PROPAGATION
9

FLOWER TIME
July — October

TOP TIPS
Use twigs to support the stems — canes can look unsightly.

HELENIUM

H. 'Coppelia'

Sneezewort

Border perennial

H. 'Butterpat'

H. 'Moerheim Beauty'

A provider of reds and yellows in the late summer herbaceous border. The daisy-like flowers have a prominent central disc — unlike Rudbeckia the petals are notched.

VARIETIES

H. 'Moerheim Beauty' – 90 cm. Copper-red.
H. 'Butterpat' – 90 cm. Yellow.
H. 'Bruno' – 1.2 m. Red.
H. 'Coppelia' – 90 cm. Orange/red.
H. 'Waldtraut' – 90 cm. Orange-brown.
H. 'Crimson Beauty' – 60 cm. Red.
H. hoopesii – 1 m. Yellow. Early.

SITE & SOIL
3

PROPAGATION
2

FLOWER TIME
July — September

TOP TIPS
Mulch in spring — stake tall varieties. Divide every few years.

HELIANTHEMUM

H. 'Wisley Primrose'

Rock Rose

Rockery perennial

H. 'Ben Hope'

One of the best plants for providing a sheet of long-lasting colour in summer. Each flower lasts for only a day or two, but new ones are borne in profusion.

VARIETIES

The usual height is 8 cm. Numerous varieties are available:
H. 'Wisley Primrose' – Yellow.
H. 'Ben Hope' – Salmon-pink.
H. 'Raspberry Ripple' – White/purplish pink.
There are a few dwarfs:
H. nummularium 'Amy Baring' – 4 cm. Yellow.

SITE & SOIL
1

PROPAGATION
10

FLOWER TIME
May — July

TOP TIPS
Can become straggly — cut back hard once the first flush has faded.

HELIANTHUS

H. 'Soleil d'Or'

Perennial Sunflower

Border perennial

H. 'Loddon Gold'

The perennial varieties of Helianthus are less popular than the giant-flowering annual ones, but they are still a good choice for the back of the border. Most are hard to find.

VARIETIES

H. 'Loddon Gold' – 1.5 m. Yellow. Double.
H. 'Monarch' – 2 m. Yellow. Semi-double.
H. 'Soleil d'Or' – 2 m. Yellow. Semi-double.
H. 'Capenoch Star' – 2 m. Yellow. Double. Quilled petals.
H. salicifolius – 2.2 m. Yellow.

SITE & SOIL
2

PROPAGATION
2

FLOWER TIME
August — October

TOP TIPS
Support flower stems. Lift and divide clumps every 3 years.

HELIANTHUS

H. annuus
'Teddy Bear'
Annual Sunflower

Bedding plant:
hardy annual

H. annuus

For garden display it is better to choose one of the compact varieties than the familiar giant. They are usually more colourful and can be seen at close quarters.

VARIETIES

H. annuus – 30 cm-3 m. Yellow. The basic species — check variety height before you buy.
H. a. 'Giant Yellow' – 1.8-3 m. Yellow. Typical giant variety.
H. a. 'Autumn Beauty' – 1.2-1.5 m. Yellow/orange/red.
H. a. 'Pacino' – 60 cm. Yellow.
H. a. 'Teddy Bear' – 60 cm. Yellow.

SITE & SOIL
2

PROPAGATION
9

FLOWER TIME
July — October

TOP TIPS
Stake tall plants — feed giant varieties weekly for maximum size.

HELICHRYSUM

H. bracteatum
'Hot Bikini'
Straw Flower

Bedding plant:
hardy annual

H. bracteatum

The most popular of the group of 'everlasting' flowers which look like double daisies and have strawy petals. For drying cut the stems just before the flowers are fully open.

VARIETIES

Several varieties of **H. bracteatum** are available:
H. b. 'Monstrosum Double Mixed' – 90 cm. Various. A tall variety with 5 cm wide flowers.
H. b. 'Hot Bikini' – 30 cm. Red/ yellow. The brightest variety.
H. b. 'Pastel Mixed' – 30 cm. Pale shades — pink, salmon etc.

SITE & SOIL
2

PROPAGATION
9

FLOWER TIME
July — September

TOP TIPS
Does not like root disturbance — best sown where it is to flower.

HELIOPHILA

H. longifolia
Heliophila

Bedding plant:
hardy annual

H. longifolia

You should be able to find seeds of this uncommon bedding plant at a large garden centre. The blooms have the four-petal arrangement of the cress family.

VARIETIES

H. longifolia (H. coronopifolia) – 30 cm. White- or yellow-eyed blue. The papery-petalled flowers are borne in clusters. Use for flower arranging — dry flowers and pods for winter decoration.
H. l. 'Blue Bird' – 30 cm. Bright blue. The only variety you are likely to find.

SITE & SOIL
2

PROPAGATION
9

FLOWER TIME
July — September

TOP TIPS
For maximum effect scatter the seeds where they are to grow.

HELIOPSIS

Heliopsis

Border perennial

H. scabra
'Golden Plume'

Heliopsis has three points in its favour among the yellow daisies. The plants are compact, they do not have to be divided every few years and the flowers are long-lasting.

VARIETIES

H. scabra – 1 m. Yellow or orange. This is the basic species. There are several varieties, but none is popular.

H. s. 'Summer Sun' – 90 cm. Yellow.

H. s. 'Golden Plume' – 1.2 m. Yellow. Favourite double variety.

H. s. 'Goldgreenheart' – 90 cm. Yellow/green. Lime-centred novelty.

SITE & SOIL
11

PROPAGATION
2

FLOWER TIME
July — August

TOP TIPS
A no-trouble plant — just cut down the stems to ground level in autumn.

HELIOTROPIUM

H. peruvianum
'Marine'

Heliotrope

Bedding plant: half-hardy annual

H. peruvianum

A favourite plant in Victorian times but not any more. Each flower is tiny, but they are massed in large heads. Fragrant, but not as sweet-smelling as it used to be.

VARIETIES

H. peruvianum – 30-45 cm. The only species. There are varieties in white, blue or purple.

H. p. 'Marine' – 45 cm. Blue-purple. 15 cm wide flower-heads.

H. p. 'Mini Marine' – 35 cm. Blue-purple. Dark green wrinkled leaves.

H. p. 'White Lady' – 30 cm. White.

H. p. 'Lord Roberts' – 30 cm. Violet.

SITE & SOIL
2

PROPAGATION
19

FLOWER TIME
June — September

TOP TIPS
Useful in the wildlife garden — very attractive to butterflies.

HELIPTERUM

H. roseum

Everlasting Flower

Hardy annual

H. roseum

Strawy-petalled daisy-like flowers on slender stems — one of the 'everlasting' flowers which can be dried for winter decoration. Cut before the flowers are fully open.

VARIETIES

H. roseum – 40 cm. White or pink. The usual species — generally sold as a mixture. May be listed as **Acroclinum**. For dried flowers, tie in bunches and hang upside-down in a cool dark place.

H. r. 'Goliath' – 40 cm. Dark-centred pink.

H. humboldtianum – 45 cm. Yellow.

SITE & SOIL
2

PROPAGATION
21

FLOWER TIME
July — September

TOP TIPS
Dislikes root disturbance. Sow the seeds where they are to flower.

HELLEBORUS

H. niger

Hellebore

Border perennial

H. orientalis

The deeply-lobed leaves provide good ground cover and the flowering time ranges from mid winter to late spring. Hellebores take a long time to recover if dug up and divided.

VARIETIES

H. niger – 30 cm. White. January-March. Christmas Rose.

H. orientalis – 45 cm. White, yellow, pink or purple. March. Lenten Rose.

H. foetidus – 45 cm. Purple-rimmed yellow. February-April. Stinking Hellebore.

H. corsicus – 60 cm. Green. April.

SITE & SOIL
15

PROPAGATION
13

FLOWER TIME
Depends on species

TOP TIPS
Dig in compost before planting — watch for slugs in spring.

HEMEROCALLIS

H. 'Bonanza'

Day Lily

Border perennial

H. 'Stafford'

Branching flower stalks rise above clumps of strap-like leaves in summer. Each bloom usually lasts for only a day but new ones continue to appear for many weeks.

VARIETIES

There are scores of Hemerocallis hybrids offered for sale.

H. 'Bonanza' – 90 cm. Yellow/red.

H. 'Stafford' – 75 cm. Red/yellow.

H. 'Pink Damask' – 75 cm. Pink/yellow.

H. 'Golden Chimes' – 60 cm. Yellow.

H. 'Black Magic' – 90 cm. Dark red.

SITE & SOIL
3

PROPAGATION
2

FLOWER TIME
June — August

TOP TIPS
Easy, but you must water thoroughly when the weather is dry.

HESPERIS

H. matronalis

Sweet Rocket

Border perennial

Hardy annual

H. matronalis
'Lilacina Flore Pleno'

A welcome contribution to the border where fragrance is important. Spikes of four-petalled flowers are borne on slender stems. The lance-shaped leaves are evergreen.

VARIETIES

H. matronalis – 60 cm. White, pink or mauve. The flower-heads are about 30 cm tall and the 1.5 cm wide blooms are attractive to butterflies. Can be invasive.

H. m. 'Albiflora' – 60 cm. White.

H. m. 'Lilacina Flore Pleno' – 60 cm. Pale lilac. Double.

H. m. 'Candiflora' – 60 cm. White.

SITE & SOIL
3

PROPAGATION
12/21

FLOWER TIME
June — July

TOP TIPS
Deteriorates with age — grow as an annual or replace every few years.

HEUCHERA

H. 'Pewter Moon'
Coral Flower

Border perennial

Heuchera, Tellima and Tiarella are ground-covers. They can be confused at the all-leaf stage but not when in flower — Heuchera blooms are bells in loose sprays.

H. sanguinea

VARIETIES

H. sanguinea – 60 cm. Pink. Silver-marbled green leaves.
H. 'Red Spangles' – 60 cm. Red.
H. 'Pewter Moon' – 40 cm. Pink. Grey-marbled green leaves.
H. micrantha diversifolia 'Palace Purple' – 50 cm. White. Bronze-purple leaves.
H. 'Rachel' – 30 cm. Pink.

SITE & SOIL
2

PROPAGATION
3

FLOWER TIME
June — August

TOP TIPS
Lift clumps every few years — divide and then replant.

HIBISCUS

H. 'Disco Belle'
Hibiscus

Bedding plant: half-hardy annual

Unlike their perennial relatives the annual varieties are not popular. The flowers live for only a day but they appear freely for many weeks. Seed pods are attractive.

H. trionum

VARIETIES

H. trionum – 60 cm. Dark-centred white or cream.
H. 'Disco Belle' – 60 cm. Various. 15 cm wide flowers. The half-hardy annual you are most likely to find.
H. 'Coppertone' – 1 m. Purple-red. Grown mainly for its copper-purple maple-like leaves.
H. 'Vanilla Ice' – 75 cm. Cream.

SITE & SOIL
1

PROPAGATION
19

FLOWER TIME
July — September

TOP TIPS
Choose a sheltered spot — Hibiscus is a tender plant. Watch for greenfly.

HOSTA

H. sieboldiana 'Elegans'
Plantain Lily

Border perennial

Grown for its spikes of trumpet-shaped flowers and its attractive leaves, often variegated or distinctly coloured. Thrives in the partial shade under trees.

H. ventricosa

VARIETIES

H. 'Royal Standard' – 60 cm. White. Tolerates deep shade.
H. ventricosa – 50 cm. Lilac.
H. sieboldiana 'Elegans' – 30 cm. Lilac-tinged white. Bluish-green leaves.
H. 'Piedmont Gold' – 50 cm. White. Yellow leaves — needs some sun.
H. fortunei – 50 cm. Mauve.

SITE & SOIL
5

PROPAGATION
6

FLOWER TIME
June — August

TOP TIPS
Dig in organic matter before planting. Protect the plants against slugs.

HYACINTHUS

Bulb

H. 'Delft Blue'

Hyacinth

A good garden bulb, but it has never achieved the outdoor popularity of narcissi, tulips and crocuses. Bulbs will overwinter in most soils. Plant 15 cm deep in autumn.

VARIETIES

H. orientalis – 25-30 cm. This species has produced hundreds of varieties — the Dutch Hybrids.
H. 'Jan Bos' – Red. Early.
H. 'Pink Pearl' – Pink. Early.
H. 'Delft Blue' – Blue. Mid-season.
H. 'L'Innocence' – White. Mid-season.
H. 'City of Haarlem' – Yellow. Late.

H. 'Pink Pearl'

SITE & SOIL
3

PROPAGATION
28

FLOWER TIME
April — May

TOP TIPS
Plant medium-sized bulbs — not the large ones used in bowls.

IBERIS

Rockery perennial

I. sempervirens

I. sempervirens 'Snowflake'

Perennial Candytuft

Popular in the rockery — evergreen, hardy and easy to grow. Give it room to spread. Flowers cover the foliage — each bloom has two long petals and two short ones.

VARIETIES

I. sempervirens – 20 cm. White. The popular species — spread 60 cm, flower clusters 5 cm across.
I. s. 'Snowflake' – 25 cm. White. Grow this variety rather than the species.
I. s. 'Little Gem' – 10 cm. White. Grow where space is limited.
I. saxatile – 10 cm. White.

SITE & SOIL
2

PROPAGATION
10

FLOWER TIME
May — June

TOP TIPS
Dead-head regularly to extend the flowering period.

IBERIS

Hardy annual

I. umbellata

I. umbellata 'Fairy Mixed'

Annual Candytuft

Few annuals are easier to grow — just sprinkle the seed in spring over the ground where it is to flower. Use it as an edging plant or for the front of the border.

VARIETIES

I. umbellata is the basic species:
I. u. 'Fairy Mixed' – 15-20 cm. Various. Pastel colours.
I. u. 'Flash Mixed' – 20-35 cm. Various. Bright colours.
I. u. 'Red Flash' – 25 cm. Red.
I. u. 'White Pinnacle' – 35 cm. White. A hyacinth-flowered candytuft with crowded spikes of blooms.

SITE & SOIL
2

PROPAGATION
21

FLOWER TIME
May — July

TOP TIPS
An excellent 'starter' plant for young children new to gardening.

IMPATIENS   Busy Lizzie

Bedding plant:
half-hardy annual

I. 'Super Elfin'

I. 'Novette Star'

I. 'Rosette'

Busy Lizzie is one of the top ten bedding plants in both Britain and the U.S, but it was not until the late 1970s that it became available as a bedding plant. Only Begonia semperflorens can rival its ability to provide sheets of colour in shade, but shade isn't essential — Impatiens will stay in flower for months in a sunny situation. Once there were only whites, pinks and reds, but now there are lilac and orange flowers plus bicolours, doubles and bright-leaved New Guinea hybrids. Difficult to raise from seed.

I. 'Blitz 2000'

I. 'Fanfare'

VARIETIES

The hybrids of **I. walleriana** fall into several groups:

Green-leaf, single, self-colours – 20 cm. Various. Included here are **I. 'Accent'** and **I. 'Super Elfin'** series. For larger flowers and taller plants choose **I. 'Blitz 2000'**.

Green-leaf, single, bicolours – 20 cm. Red/white. Included here are **I. 'Novette Star'** and **I. 'Starbright'**.

Bronzy leaves – 20 cm. **I. 'Deco'**.

Picotee flowers – 20 cm. **I. 'Swirls'**.

Double flowers – 25 cm. Included here are **I. 'Carousel'** and **I. 'Rosette'**. Some will be singles.

New Guinea Hybrids – 30-45 cm. Multicoloured leaves. Included here are **I. 'Tango'** and **I. 'Fanfare'**.

SITE & SOIL
4

PROPAGATION
25

FLOWER TIME
June — October

TOP TIPS
Add organic material to the soil before planting. Do not plant out before the end of May or early June. Water thoroughly in dry weather. Lift and keep indoors during winter.

IMPATIENS

I. balsamina
'Tom Thumb'

Balsam

Bedding plant:
half-hardy annual

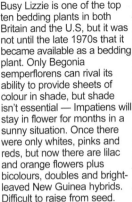

I. balsamina

A close relative of Busy Lizzie but there are two important differences — Balsam needs full sun to thrive and it does not do well in cool and wet summers. No longer popular.

VARIETIES

I. **balsamina** is the basic species. Blooms borne on stems between leaves — sometimes half-hidden.

I. b. **'Camellia-flowered'** – 45 cm. Various. Double.

I. b. **'Tom Thumb'** – 20 cm. Various. Double.

I. b. **'Topknot'** – 30 cm. Various. Double. Flowers held above leaves.

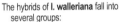

SITE & SOIL
1

PROPAGATION
7

FLOWER TIME
July — October

TOP TIPS
Pinch back taller types to induce bushiness. Thin leaves to show flowers.

INCARVILLEA

I. mairei

Chinese Trumpet Flower

Border perennial

An unusual plant with an exotic appearance. The flower stalks bearing gloxinia-like blooms emerge in late spring before the leaves. All growth disappears in winter.

VARIETIES

I. **delavayi** – 60 cm. Dark pink. 8 cm wide flowers. Dark green ferny leaves. Most popular type.

I. **d. 'Bees Pink'** – 60 cm. Pale pink.

I. **mairei** – 40 cm. Yellow-throated rose-red. Leaves not ferny.

I. **m. 'Grandiflora'** – 20 cm. Pink.

I. **m. 'Frank Ludlow'** – 10 cm. Dark pink.

I. delavayi

SITE & SOIL
1

PROPAGATION
13

FLOWER TIME
May — June

TOP TIPS
Add compost to the soil before planting. Mulch crowns in winter.

INULA

I. orientalis

Inula

Border perennial
Rockery perennial

There are many yellow daisy-like perennials for the border — choose this uncommon one if you have a partially shady site in heavy soil or if you like finely-rayed flowers.

VARIETIES

I. **hookeri** – 60 cm. Yellow. 8 cm wide flowers. Central disc turns brown with age. Spreads rapidly.

I. **orientalis** – 60 cm. Yellow. Less invasive than I. hookeri.

I. **ensifolia 'Compacta'** – 10 cm. Yellow. Dwarf for the rock garden.

I. **magnifica** – 2 m. Yellow. Giant for the back of the border.

I. hookeri

SITE & SOIL
10

PROPAGATION
2

FLOWER TIME
July — August

TOP TIPS
Apply a mulch around stems in spring. Water in dry weather.

IPHEION

I. 'Rolf Fiedler'

Spring Starflower

Bulb

A trouble-free fragrant bulb for the rockery, woodland garden or front of the border. Several stalks topped with starry flowers appear above the strap-like leaves.

VARIETIES

I. **uniflorum** – 15 cm. Pale blue. 3 cm wide flowers. Crushed leaves emit garlic odour.

I. **u. 'Album'** – 15 cm. White.

I. **u. 'Wisley Blue'** – 15 cm. Violet.

I. **u. 'Froyle Mill'** – 15 cm. Dark violet.

I. **'Rolf Fiedler'** – 10 cm. Brightest of all the violets but also the most tender.

I. uniflorum

SITE & SOIL
3

PROPAGATION
3

FLOWER TIME
April — May

TOP TIPS
Avoid an exposed site — prolonged frosts can be damaging.

IPOMOEA

I. tricolor

Morning Glory

Bedding plant: half-hardy annual

The wiry stems twine around upright supports and the trumpet-shaped flowers appear in summer. Each flower lasts for only one day but they are borne continually.

VARIETIES

I. **purpurea** (**Convolvulus major**) – 2.5-3 m. White-throated purple.
I. **tricolor** – 3 m. White-throated blue.
I. t. **'Heavenly Blue'** – 3 m. White-throated blue.
I. t. **'Flying Saucers'** – 3 m. White-striped blue.
I. t. **'Cardinal'** – 3 m. White-throated red.

I. tricolor 'Heavenly Blue'

SITE & SOIL
2

PROPAGATION
25

FLOWER TIME
July — September

TOP TIPS
Damaged by cold winds — choose a sunny and sheltered site.

IRIS

I. 'Arctic Fancy'

Bearded Iris

Border perennial
Rockery perennial

Most Irises spread by rhizomes (thickened horizontal stems) — most popular are the Bearded Irises. The flowers have fleshy hairs (beard) on the outer petals (falls).

VARIETIES

Tall group – 75 cm or over. June.
  Example: I. **'Jane Phillips'** (Blue).
Intermediate group – 45-75 cm. May.
  Example: I. **'Arctic Fancy'** (Blue/white).
Dwarf group – 20-45 cm. May.
  Example: I. **'Pygmy Gold'** (Gold).
Miniature group – Up to 20 cm. April.
  Example: I. **pumila** (Various).

I. 'Jane Phillips'

SITE & SOIL
1

PROPAGATION
29

FLOWER TIME
Depends on variety

TOP TIPS
Plant when soil is moist — leave top half of rhizome uncovered.

IRIS

I. unguicularis

Beardless Iris

Border perennial
Bog plant

Differs from the more popular Bearded Irises by having hairless outer petals (falls) and by having rhizomes which generally grow underground and not partly on the surface.

VARIETIES

Pacific Coast Irises. Evergreen.
  Example: I. **innominata** (Yellow/brown).
Siberian Irises. Grassy leaves.
  Example: I. **sibirica 'Perry's Blue'**.
Winter Irises. November-March.
  Example: I. **unguicularis** (Violet).
Water Irises. Boggy ground needed.
  Example: I. **laevigata** (Blue).

I. innominata

SITE & SOIL
3

PROPAGATION
29

FLOWER TIME
Depends on species

TOP TIPS
Plant the rhizomes 3-5 cm deep — trim top off the leaves.

IRIS

Bulb Iris

Bulb

I. 'Lemon Queen'

I. reticulata

The Bulb Irises are generally smaller than the Rhizome ones — these are plants for the rockery or front of the border. Wait for at least 4-5 years before dividing.

VARIETIES

Reticulata Irises – 8-15 cm. February-March. These are popular rockery plants.
   I. danfordiae – Brown/yellow.
   I. reticulata – Yellow/purple.
Xiphium Irises – 50 cm. June-July.
   I. 'Lemon Queen' – Yellow.
   I. 'Wedgwood' – Blue.
   I. xiphium – Blue-violet.

SITE & SOIL
18

PROPAGATION
3

FLOWER TIME
Depends on variety

TOP TIPS
All need light soil. Check winter hardiness before buying.

KNIPHOFIA

Red Hot Poker

K. 'Springtime'

Border perennial

K. 'Royal Standard'

Easy to recognise — grassy leaves and spikes of long tubular flowers. Some but not all have the traditional red hot poker appearance — red-tipped yellow flower-heads.

VARIETIES

K. uvaria – 75 cm-1.5 m. Various. Parent species of many hybrids:
For a true poker choose **K. 'Royal Standard'** or **K. 'Springtime'**.
For single colours choose **K. 'Ice Queen'** (Cream), **K. 'Bees' Sunset'** (Orange) or **K. 'Little Maid'** (Cream. Dwarf).
K. galpinii – 45 cm. Orange.

SITE & SOIL
2

PROPAGATION
6

FLOWER TIME
July — September

TOP TIPS
On exposed sites cover the crowns with peat or straw in winter.

LAMIUM

Dead Nettle

L. maculatum

Border perennial

L. maculatum 'Beacon Silver'

The evergreen leaves of this ground cover plant are usually striped or splashed with silver and are the main reason for its choice. The floral display in early summer is a bonus.

VARIETIES

L. maculatum – 25 cm. Various. The most popular species.
L. m. 'Beacon Silver' – 25 cm. Pink. Green-edged silver leaves.
L. m. 'White Nancy' – 25 cm. White. Green-edged silver leaves.
L. m. 'Aureum' – 25 cm. Pink. White-centred yellow leaves.
L. galeobdolon – 60 cm. Yellow.

SITE & SOIL
5

PROPAGATION
2

FLOWER TIME
May — July

TOP TIPS
Can be invasive — cut back after flowering is over.

LATHYRUS

Sweet Pea

Bedding plant: hardy annual

L. odoratus 'Leamington'

L. odoratus 'Knee-hi'

SITE & SOIL
2

PROPAGATION
27/30

Many varieties appeared in Victorian catalogues, but the range nowadays is much greater. Of course the tall ones remain the favourite group, but you can buy knee-high ones and even dwarfs which do not require support. The colour range is vast — only the true yellows are missing. Unfortunately some of the fragrance has been lost in the modern types, and so many gardeners prefer the small-flowered ones which are renowned for their scent. Use for screening and growing through old trees.

L. odoratus 'Winston Churchill'

VARIETIES

L. odoratus is the basic species. The Tall group (1.5-2.4 m) dominate the catalogues. The Spencer varieties with large frilly petals are the most popular – **'Winston Churchill'** (Red), **'Leamington'** (Mauve), **'Swan Lake'** (White). For fragrance choose **'Old-fashioned Mixture'** (Various) or **'Painted Lady'** (Red/white). For maximum flowers per stem buy **'Royal'**, **'Bouquet'** or **'Galaxy'** strains.

The Intermediate group (60-90 cm) need little support – **'Knee-hi'** (Various), **'Jet Set'** (Various).

The Dwarf group (15-45 cm) are not climbers – **'Bijou'** (Various), **'Pink Cupid'** (Pink/white).

L. odoratus 'Bijou'

FLOWER TIME
June — September

TOP TIPS
Soak seeds overnight before sowing. Pinch out tips when seedlings are about 10 cm high. Provide support and water in dry weather. Dead-head regularly.

LATHYRUS

Everlasting Pea

Border perennial

L. latifolius 'White Pearl'

L. grandiflorus

SITE & SOIL
3

PROPAGATION
13

Sweet Peas are by far the most popular type of Lathyrus, but they are not the only ones. The perennial species are climbers which deserve to be more widely grown.

VARIETIES

L. grandiflorus – 1.5 m. Pink-purple. Everlasting Pea. Spreading climber. July-September.

L. latifolius 'White Pearl' – 1.8 m. White. Perennial Pea. Spreading climber. July-September.

L. verna – 45 cm. Purple. Spring Vetch. Non-climbing bush. April-May.

FLOWER TIME
Depends on species

TOP TIPS
Dislikes root disturbance — do not lift and divide established plants.

LAURENTIA

L. axillaris 'Fantasy Blue'
Laurentia

Bedding plant: half-hardy annual

Rare until the 1990s, but now you will find seeds in the catalogues and seedlings at the garden centre in spring. Each fine-leaved dome bears masses of starry flowers.

VARIETIES

L. axillaris (**Solenopsis axillaris**) – 25 cm. Various. Narrow-petalled 3 cm wide flowers. The only species you will find — several varieties are available:

L. a. '**Blue Star**' (Blue).
L. a. '**Fantasy Blue**' (Blue).
L. a. '**Mill Toy**' (Mauve).
L. a. '**Pink Charm**' (Pink).

L. axillaris 'Pink Charm'

SITE & SOIL
1

PROPAGATION
7

FLOWER TIME
June — October

TOP TIPS
Wear gloves when handling — the leaves can irritate the skin.

LAVATERA

L. trimestris 'Mont Blanc'
Annual Mallow

Hardy annual

There are modern varieties of this old cottage garden plant which are bold and bright enough to hold their own next to showy perennials in the border.

VARIETIES

L. trimestris – 1 m. Pink. There are several excellent varieties:
L. t. '**Loveliness**' – 1 m. Pink.
L. t. '**Mont Blanc**' – 60 cm. White.
L. t. '**Silver Cup**' – 75 cm. Pink. Popular. Very free flowering.
L. t. '**Ruby Regis**' – 60 cm. Rose-red.
L. t. '**Beauty Mixed**' – 60 cm. Rose, pink or white.

L. trimestris 'Silver Cup'

SITE & SOIL
3

PROPAGATION
21

FLOWER TIME
July — September

TOP TIPS
Choose a sheltered spot. Stake tall varieties and dead-head regularly.

LEONTOPODIUM

L. alpinum
Edelweiss

Rockery perennial

A symbol of the Alps which will grow quite happily in a well-drained lowland rockery. The curious flowers are interesting rather than beautiful.

VARIETIES

L. alpinum – 15 cm. Greyish-white. The narrow leaves are hoary above — densely woolly below. Flower-heads have a central group of rayless daisy-like flowers surrounded by flannel-like bracts.
L. a. '**Mignon**' – 15 cm. Greyish-white. Longer-living than the species.

L. alpinum

SITE & SOIL
1

PROPAGATION
7

FLOWER TIME
June — July

TOP TIPS
Incorporate grit or coarse sand into the soil before planting.

LEUCANTHEMUM

Border perennial

L. superbum
'Wirral Supreme'

L. superbum
'Esther Read'
Shasta Daisy

Chrysanthemum used to be the Latin name of this border plant. The Shasta Daisy bears large flowers — the petals are white and the centres are yellow.

VARIETIES

L. superbum – 1 m. White. 5-10 cm wide flowers.
L. s. 'Wirral Supreme' – 90 cm. White. Semi-double. Popular.
L. s. 'Esther Read' – 60 cm. White. Double. Popular.
L. s. 'Snowcap' – 20 cm. White. Single. The best dwarf.
L. s. 'Alaska' – 70 cm. White. Single.

FLOWER TIME
June — August

TOP TIPS
Divide plants every 3 years. Mulch in May — cut down in autumn.

LEUCOJUM

Bulb

L. vernum

L. aestivum
Snowflake

Snowdrops and Snowflakes have flowers with six white petals, but Snowflake petals are all the same size and all are green- or yellow-spotted at the tips.

VARIETIES

There are spring-, summer- and autumn-flowering types.
L. vernum – 20 cm. Green-tipped white. February-March.
L. v. 'Carpathicum' – 20 cm. Yellow-tipped white. February-March.
L. aestivum – 60 cm. April-May.
L. autumnale – 12 cm. Red-based white. September. Needs full sun.

FLOWER TIME
Depends on species

TOP TIPS
Support flower stalks with twigs. Let leaves die down naturally.

LEWISIA

Rockery perennial

L. cotyledon

L. cotyledon
Lewisia

Flowers in pink, peach, orange or white with petals which are often striped. Unfortunately it is not easy to keep as water in the crown causes it to rot in winter.

VARIETIES

L. cotyledon – 25 cm. Various. Evergreen. Several showy hybrids are available, such as **'Sunset'** and **'Ashwood Ruby'**.
L. tweedyi – 20 cm. White or peach. Evergreen. Large 8 cm wide flowers.
L. rediviva – 5 cm. White or pink. Deciduous.

FLOWER TIME
May — June

TOP TIPS
Plant it sideways in a crevice between rocks or bricks.

X

LIATRIS

Border perennial

L. spicata

SITE & SOIL
3

PROPAGATION
2

L. spicata 'Kobold'

Gayfeather

Erect spikes are densely clothed with small fluffy flowers in white, pink or pale purple. An unusual feature is that the blooms open from the top of the spike downwards.

VARIETIES

L. spicata – 1.2 m. Pale purple. The basic species. Flower spike is about 50 cm long.

L. s. 'Floristan Weiss' – 90 cm. White.

L. s. 'Floristan Violett' – 90 cm. Purple.

L. s. 'Kobold' – 60 cm. Mauve. Best choice where space is limited.

FLOWER TIME
July — September

TOP TIPS
Add compost before planting and water in dry weather.

LIBERTIA

Border perennial

L. formosa

Libertia

Evergreens are much less common among hardy perennials than with shrubs and trees, so it is worth considering this one for the herbaceous border.

L. grandiflora

VARIETIES

L. formosa – 75 cm. White. Flowers have 3 large outer petals and 3 small inner ones. In autumn showy brown seed heads appear.

SITE & SOIL
1

PROPAGATION
6

L. grandiflora – 75 cm. White. Similar to L. formosa, but leaves turn brown in winter.

L. caerulescens – 60 cm. Pale blue. Not easy to find.

FLOWER TIME
May — July

TOP TIPS
Enrich the soil with compost or old manure before planting.

LIGULARIA

Border perennial
Bog plant

L. dentata

SITE & SOIL
15

PROPAGATION
2

L. 'The Rocket'

Golden Rays

Ligularia needs space, water-retentive soil and some shade. The large leaves cover the ground and smother weeds, and in summer the yellow or orange flowers appear.

VARIETIES

L. dentata – 90 cm. Golden-yellow. 10 cm wide flowers.

L. d. 'Desdemona' – 90 cm. Orange. Brownish-green leaves.

L. d. 'Othello' – 90 cm. Orange.

L. 'The Rocket' – 1.5 m. Yellow. Small flowers on erect black-stalked spikes.

L. 'Gregynog Gold' – 1.8 m. Yellow.

FLOWER TIME
July — September

TOP TIPS
Water copiously in dry weather. Lift and divide every 3 years.

LILIUM

Bulb

Turk's-cap shaped Lily

Trumpet shaped Lily

Bowl shaped Lily

SITE & SOIL
3

PROPAGATION
1

Hybrid Lily

Various species of Lilies have been grown in gardens for thousands of years, but it was the introduction of the Hybrid Lilies in the 20th century which set new standards for size, vigour and disease resistance. Most grow to 1-1.5 m, but dwarf varieties such as the Pixie strain have become a common sight in bud or flower at the garden centre in June. Tall varieties will need staking and faded blooms should be removed. Cut down the stems to ground level in autumn and apply a mulch of peat or leaf mould.

VARIETIES

There are thousands of varieties. Favourites include:

Mid-Century Hybrids – Bowl shaped. June-July. **L. 'Enchantment'** (Red), **L. 'Destiny'** (Yellow), **L. 'Cinnabar'** (Maroon).

Pixie Hybrids – Bowl shaped. June-July. **L. 'Orange Pixie'** (Golden yellow).

Trumpet Hybrids – Trumpet shaped. July-August. **L. 'African Queen'** (Orange).

Bellingham Hybrids – Turk's-cap shaped. July. **L. 'Shuksan'** (Brown-spotted yellow).

Oriental Hybrids – Bowl shaped. August-September. **L. 'Stargazer'** (White-edged pink).

L. 'Cinnabar'

L. 'Shuksan'

FLOWER TIME
Depends on variety

TOP TIPS
Plant bulbs immediately on arrival — do not let them dry out. Put coarse sand in the hole. Water thoroughly in dry weather. Do not hoe close to stems.

LILIUM

Bulb

L. martagon

SITE & SOIL
3

PROPAGATION
1

L. regale

Species Lily

Far fewer types are available compared with the Hybrid Lilies, but there are many beautiful ~~old~~ ones here. Some are hard to grow. Good drainage is essential.

VARIETIES

Favourites include:

L. regale – 1.2 m. White. Trumpet shaped. July.

L. martagon – 1 m. Pink-purple. Turk's-cap shaped. July.

L. tigrinum – 1.5 m. Black-spotted orange. Turk's-cap shaped. August.

L. candidum – 1 m. White. Trumpet shaped. July.

FLOWER TIME
Depends on species

TOP TIPS
For tips see Hybrid Lily notes above. Most dislike lime.

LIMNANTHES
L. douglasii
Poached Egg Flower

Hardy annual

L. douglasii

Alyssum and Lobelia are seen everywhere as edging plants for the front of the border — Limnanthes makes a welcome change. The two-toned flowers are abundant.

VARIETIES

L. douglasii – 15 cm. Yellow petals with a white edge — hence the common name. This is the only species you will find — it is in most seed catalogues. Easy to grow — 2 cm wide flowers cover almost all the foliage when grown in full sun. Fragrance is sweet but not strong. Leaves are pale green and ferny.

FLOWER TIME
June — October

TOP TIPS
Grow it if you wish to attract bees to your border.

LIMONIUM
L. latifolium
Sea Lavender

Border perennial

L. latifolium

SITE & SOIL
2

PROPAGATION
12

Sea Lavender is a dual-purpose plant — grow it to produce a summer-long display of tiny blooms and cut it to provide a supply of 'everlasting' flowers for drying.

VARIETIES

L. latifolium (Statice latifolia) – 60 cm. Lavender. The basic perennial species. Cut stems just before flowers open and hang upside-down in a dry place.
L. l. 'Blue Cloud' – 60 cm. Lavender.
L. l. 'Violetta' – 60 cm. Dark violet.
L. l. 'Collyers Pink' – 60 cm. Pink.
L. l. 'Robert Butler' – 45 cm. Violet.

FLOWER TIME
July — September

TOP TIPS
Do not lift and divide — take cuttings to increase your stock.

LIMONIUM
L. sinuatum
Statice

Bedding plant: half-hardy annual

L. sinuatum

SITE & SOIL
2

PROPAGATION
7

The most popular of the 'everlasting' flowers — for the drying method see Sea Lavender above. Winged stems bear clusters of tiny papery-petalled flowers.

VARIETIES

L. sinuatum – 45 cm. Various.
L. s. 'Sunset Shades' – 45 cm. Various.
L. s. 'Petite Bouquet' – 30 cm. Various.
L. s. 'Blue Peter' – 45 cm. Blue.
L. s. 'Gold Coast' – 45 cm. Yellow.
L. suworowii – 45 cm. Pink. Not for drying.

FLOWER TIME
July — September

TOP TIPS
For drying cut stems just before the flowers are fully open.

LINARIA

Border perennial
• Rockery perennial

L. alpina

SITE & SOIL
2

PROPAGATION
6

L. purpurea 'Canon Went'

Toadflax

You will not find the perennial Linaria at every garden centre, but it is easy to grow. Snapdragon-like flowers appear over many months. Tends to be short-lived.

VARIETIES

L. purpurea – 70 cm. Purple. Most popular species.
L. p. 'Canon Went' – 60 cm. Pink. Most popular variety.
L. p. 'Springside White' – 45 cm. White.
L. vulgaris – 60 cm. Yellow/orange.
L. alpina – 15 cm. Violet/orange. Flowers borne in clusters.

FLOWER TIME
May — September

TOP TIPS
Can become a nuisance as it self-seeds very readily.

LINUM

Border perennial
• Rockery perennial

L. perenne

SITE & SOIL
2

PROPAGATION
10

L. narbonense

Perennial Flax

The wiry stems with narrow leaves give these plants a delicate appearance. The 5-petalled blooms last for only a day, but during summer there are always more buds to open.

VARIETIES

L. perenne – 30 cm. Various.
L. p. 'Blue Sapphire' – 30 cm. Blue.
L. p. 'Alpinum' – 15 cm. Sky blue.
L. narbonense – 45 cm. White-centred.
L. n. 'Heavenly Blue' – 30 cm. White-centred blue.
L. 'Gemmel's Hybrid' – 15 cm. Yellow. Dome-shaped dwarf.

FLOWER TIME
June — August

TOP TIPS
Mulch in spring — water during dry spells in summer.

LINUM

Hardy annual

L. grandiflorum 'Rubrum'

SITE & SOIL
2

PROPAGATION
21

L. grandiflorum 'Rubrum'

Annual Flax

A good choice if you like bright flowers which flutter in the breeze. The 5 cm wide flat-faced blooms are borne in clusters on thin stems. No value as cut flowers.

VARIETIES

L. grandiflorum – 60 cm. Pink. The parent of the annual varieties.
L. g. 'Rubrum' – 30 cm. Bright red. Satin-like petals — the most popular variety.
L. g. 'Album' – 30 cm. White.
L. g. 'Bright Eyes' – 30 cm. Red-centred white.
L. g. 'Blue Flax' – 30 cm. Blue.

FLOWER TIME
June — August

TOP TIPS
A spindly plant so grow it in large patches rather than narrow strips.

LIRIOPE

Border perennial

L. muscari

Lily Turf

Good ground cover for shade and dry areas — there are arching evergreen leaves and spikes of tiny bell-shaped flowers throughout the autumn.

VARIETIES

L. muscari – 30 cm. Mauve. The basic species.
L. m. 'Monroe White' – 30 cm. White.
L. m. 'Majestic' – 30 cm. Lavender.
L. m. 'Royal Purple' – 30 cm. Purple.
L. m. 'Variegata' – 25 cm. Lavender. White-striped green leaves.
L. spicata – 25 cm. Mauve or white.

SITE & SOIL
4

PROPAGATION
6

FLOWER TIME
September — November

TOP TIPS
Divide every few years to keep in check. Remove old leaves in spring.

LITHOSPERMUM

Rockery perennial

L. oleifolium

L. diffusum 'Heavenly Blue'

Gromwell

Ground cover for the rockery — the creeping stems clothed with narrow leaves will spread for up to 60 cm. Unlike many other rockery plants it needs a humus-rich soil.

VARIETIES

L. diffusum – 15 cm. Blue. 2 cm wide flowers. Dislikes lime.
L. d. 'Heavenly Blue' – 15 cm. Blue. The most popular variety.
L. d. 'Grace Ward' – 15 cm. Blue. Very similar to L.d. 'Heavenly Blue'.
L. oleifolium – 20 cm. Changes from pink to blue as flowers open. Silvery-grey leaves.

SITE & SOIL
9

PROPAGATION
10

FLOWER TIME
June — September

TOP TIPS
Grow L. oleifolium rather than L. diffusum if soil is chalky.

LOBELIA

Border perennial
Bog plant

L. cardinalis

L. siphilitica

Perennial Lobelia

The perennial Lobelia is quite different from its popular blue bedding relative. The usual types have 60 cm-1.5 m high stems with flower spikes in pink, red, blue or purple.

VARIETIES

L. 'Queen Victoria' – 1 m. Red. Dark red leaves.
L. cardinalis – 1 m. Red. Similar to above, but leaves are green.
L. 'Flamingo' – 1 m. Pink.
L. 'Compliment Scarlet' – 1 m. Red. Green leaves. Can be grown as a half-hardy annual.
L. siphilitica – 75 cm. Blue-purple.

SITE & SOIL
19

PROPAGATION
6

FLOWER TIME
July — August

TOP TIPS
Damp soil is essential — mulch over crowns in winter.

LOBELIA

**Bedding plant:
half-hardy annual**

*L. erinus 'Mrs.
Clibran Improved'*

SITE & SOIL

13

PROPAGATION

7

L. erinus 'Sapphire'

Annual Lobelia

Lobelias lining the edges of beds or hanging from containers are a basic feature of the summer garden, but it is not a grow-anywhere plant. Water promptly in dry weather.

VARIETIES

L. erinus – 10 cm. Blue, white or red. Varieties include:

L. e. 'Mrs. Clibran Improved' – 10 cm. White-eyed dark blue.

L. e. 'Crystal Palace' – 10 cm. Blue. Bronze leaves.

L. e. 'White Lady' – 10 cm. White.

L. e. 'Sapphire' – 10 cm. White-eyed violet. Trailing.

FLOWER TIME

June — September

TOP TIPS

Pinch out seedling tips to induce bushiness. Enrich the soil with compost.

LUNARIA

**Bedding plant:
hardy biennial**

L. annua

SITE & SOIL

5

PROPAGATION

16

L. annua 'Albiflora'

Honesty

Lunaria is not grown for the charm of its floral display — the flat seed heads which look like pearly discs are the key feature. Cut in autumn and dry indoors.

VARIETIES

L. annua – 70 cm. Purple. 1 cm wide flowers in branching sprays. Toothed leaves. The basic species with several varieties:

L. a. 'Munstead Purple' – 70 cm. Purple.

L. a. 'Albiflora' – 70 cm. White.

L. a. 'Variegata' – 70 cm. Rose-purple. Cream-edged leaves.

FLOWER TIME

April — June

TOP TIPS

Remember not to dead-head if you want the seed pods.

LUPINUS

Border perennial

L. 'Russell Hybrid'

SITE & SOIL

17

PROPAGATION

12

L. 'Monarch'

Lupin

Large spires of pea-like flowers provide bright splashes of colour in early summer. Quick-growing and cheap to buy, but they are short-lived.

VARIETIES

L. polyphyllus has produced many hybrids. The **L. 'Russell Hybrids'** are the most popular — 90 cm-1.2 m. Various.

L. 'Chandelier' – 90 cm. Yellow.

L. 'My Castle' – 90 cm. Red.

L. 'Monarch' – 90 cm. Purple/yellow.

L. 'The Governor' – 90 cm. Blue/white.

FLOWER TIME

June — July

TOP TIPS

Add compost before planting. Dead-head to induce a second flush.

LUPINUS

Annual Lupin

L. 'Lulu'

Bedding plant:
hardy annual
or
hardy perennial

*L. nanus
'Pixie Delight'*

Annual Lupins are worth trying. You will not get the height, bloom size nor bright colours of the stately perennials, but their daintiness can be an advantage.

VARIETIES

L. nanus 'Pixie Delight' – 50 cm. Various. The most popular annual.
L. texensis – 25 cm. Blue. Texas Bluebonnet.

Some dwarf perennial varieties can be grown as annuals. Examples include:

L. 'Lulu' – 60 cm. Various.
L. 'Gallery' – 50 cm. Various.

SITE & SOIL
17

PROPAGATION
9

FLOWER TIME
June — September

TOP TIPS
Humus-rich soil not necessary. Keep watch for powdery mildew.

LYCHNIS

Campion

L. chalcedonica

Border perennial
Rockery perennial

L. coronaria

Most Campions belong in the border but L. alpina is small enough to be grown in the cracks between paving stones. The petals are notched or deeply cut.

VARIETIES

L. chalcedonica – 90 cm. Red. Most popular species. Tight flower-heads on stiff stems. June-August.
L. c. 'Albiflora' – 90 cm. White.
L. arkwrightii 'Vesuvius' – 30 cm. Red. June-July.
L. coronaria – 45 cm. Pink. Loose flower sprays. July-August.
L. alpina – 10 cm. Pink. May-July.

SITE & SOIL
2

PROPAGATION
1

FLOWER TIME
Depends on species

TOP TIPS
Water thoroughly in dry weather. Dead-head to prolong display.

LYSICHITON

Skunk Cabbage

L. americanus

Bog plant

L. americanus

A bold and eye-catching plant for moist ground or the shallow edge of the pond. Despite the striking nature of the large flowers it has never become popular.

VARIETIES

L. americanus – 1 m. Yellow. Yellow Skunk Cabbage. The only species you are likely to find. 30 cm arum-like flower-heads. Leaves appear after the flowers. Crushed foliage has an unpleasant smell.
L. camtschatcensis – 60 cm. White. White Skunk Cabbage. A better choice where space is limited.

SITE & SOIL
16

PROPAGATION
6

FLOWER TIME
April

TOP TIPS
Have patience — flowers may not appear for several years.

LYSIMACHIA

Border perennial
Rockery perennial

L. nummularia
Lysimachia

L. punctata

The border species have erect stems and white or yellow flowers borne in various ways. The rockery types are quite different — trailing stems form a flower-studded carpet.

VARIETIES

L. punctata – 75 cm. Yellow. Yellow Loosestrife. Flowers in whorls. June-August.
L. ciliata – 90 cm. Yellow. Flowers borne singly. July-August.
L. clethroides – 90 cm. White. Curved spikes. July-September.
L. nummularia – 5 cm. Yellow. Creeping Jenny. May-August.

SITE & SOIL
13

PROPAGATION
2

FLOWER TIME
Depends on species

TOP TIPS
The popular species are invasive — cut back annually if necessary.

LYTHRUM

Border perennial
Bog plant

L. salicaria 'Firecandle'
Purple Loosestrife

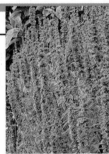

L. salicaria

A plant for the moist border or boggy land near the pool. Attractive but can be invasive, so cut down stems after flowering to prevent self-seeding.

VARIETIES

L. salicaria – 1.8 m. Pink. Narrow flower spikes are densely packed with starry blooms.
L. s. 'The Beacon' – 90 cm. Red.
L. s. 'Firecandle' – 90 cm. Rose-red.
L. s. 'Lady Sackville' – 1.2 m. Rose-red.
L. virgatum – 50 cm. Pink. Useful where space is limited.

SITE & SOIL
13

PROPAGATION
2

FLOWER TIME
June — September

TOP TIPS
Mulch in spring and water copiously in dry weather. Watch for slugs.

MACLEAYA

Border perennial

M. cordata
Plume Poppy

M. cordata

In summer large plume-like flower-heads appear above the deeply-cut leaves. Not for the small garden — it belongs at the back of an extensive herbaceous border.

VARIETIES

M. cordata – 1.8-2.4 m. Pearly white. 1 m plumes of tiny flowers. Leaves are grey-brown above and hoary white below.
M. c. 'Flamingo' – 1.8-2.4 m. Pink-tinged white.
M. microcarpa 'Kelway's Coral Plume' – 1.8-2.4 m. Pink-tinged buff. Usually sold as M. cordata.

SITE & SOIL
10

PROPAGATION
6

FLOWER TIME
July — August

TOP TIPS
Think before buying — suckers can spread rapidly into other plants.

MALCOLMIA

Hardy annual

M. maritima
Virginia Stock

Few annuals are as easy to grow as Virginia Stock — a thin scattering of seed and in a month or two the plants are in flower and remain in bloom for several weeks.

VARIETIES

M. maritima – 20 cm. White, pink, red or mauve. 1 cm wide flowers are borne on slender stems. Grows well in starved soil or in cracks between paving stones, but disappoints in a cold, rainy summer. Usually sold as a mixture, but single colours are available such as:
M.m. 'Crimson King' – 20 cm. Red.

M. maritima

SITE & SOIL
4

PROPAGATION
21

FLOWER TIME
June — October

TOP TIPS
Repeat sowings every month will produce a summer-long display.

MALOPE

Hardy annual

M. trifida
Malope

Can be confused with Lavatera — both have a bushy growth habit and bear large bowl-shaped flowers. Malope is more reliable and has a wider colour range.

VARIETIES

M. trifida – 90 cm. Pale purple. The basic species.
M.t. 'Grandiflora' – 90 cm. Crimson. Large-flowered variety — blooms are 7-10 cm across.
M.t. 'Excelsior Mixed' – 90 cm. Various. A mixture is the usual choice. Some blooms will be prominently veined.

M. trifida
'Grandiflora'

SITE & SOIL
2

PROPAGATION
21

FLOWER TIME
July — October

TOP TIPS
Grow it where an economical space-filler is required.

MALVA

Border perennial

M. moschata 'Alba'
Mallow

This border perennial is much less popular than Lavatera with which it can be easily confused — both have flowers which are large and usually bowl-shaped. Easy to grow.

VARIETIES

M. moschata – 60 cm. Pink or lavender. Musk Mallow. The species you are most likely to find.
M.m. 'Alba' – 60 cm. White.
M. sylvestris has several varieties:
M.s. 'Primley Blue' – 20 cm. Pale blue.
M.s. 'Mauritanica' – 1.5 m. Red. Large ruffled flowers.

M. sylvestris
'Primley Blue'

SITE & SOIL
2

PROPAGATION
10

FLOWER TIME
June — September

TOP TIPS
Tall varieties may need staking. Watch for self-sown seedlings.

MATTHIOLA

Annual Stock

Bedding plant: half-hardy annual

M. incana
'Ten Week Mixed'

SITE & SOIL
17

PROPAGATION
7

Stocks have lost much of their popularity but their charm remains — densely-clustered flowering spikes with a strong fragrance above soft grey-green leaves.

VARIETIES

M.incana – Ten Week Stocks:
M.i. 'Ten Week Mixed' – 30 cm. Various. Mostly double.
M.i. 'Cinderella' – 20 cm. Various. More compact and longer flowering.
M.i. 'Giant Excelsior' – 70 cm. Various.
M.bicornis – 30 cm. Lilac. Night-scented Stock. Hardy.

FLOWER TIME
June — August

TOP TIPS
Can be sown outdoors in April or May where they are to flower.

MATTHIOLA

M. incana
'Brompton Mixed'

Biennial Stock

Bedding plant: hardy biennial

M. incana
'Brompton Mixed'

SITE & SOIL
17

PROPAGATION
16

Still very popular as cut flowers but are no longer favourite bedding plants for providing spring colour. Raising all-double plants from seed is a tricky business.

VARIETIES

M. incana is the basic species:
M. i. 'Brompton Mixed' – 45 cm. Various. Bushy branching plants with clusters of fragrant flowers.
M. i. 'East Lothian Mixed' – 30 cm. Various. East Lothian Stocks look like small Brompton Stocks. Biennial — can also be grown as a hardy annual.

FLOWER TIME
April — May

TOP TIPS
Buy plants rather than seeds for an all-double flower display.

MAZUS

M. reptans

Mazus

Rockery perennial

M. reptans

SITE & SOIL
17

PROPAGATION
6

An interesting ground cover for the rockery which you should be able to find at a large garden centre. The bottom petal is spotted with white and gold.

VARIETIES

M. reptans – 5 cm. Lilac. Spreads to more than 40 cm – flowers are 2 cm long. Not recommended for alkaline soil.
M. r. 'Albus' – 5 cm. White.
M. radicans – 5 cm. Purple-centred white. Bronzy-green leaves.
M. pumilio – 5 cm. Yellow-centred white. Late flowering.

FLOWER TIME
June — August

TOP TIPS
Guard against slugs and snails in spring. Water in dry weather.

MECONOPSIS

M. cambrica
Meconopsis

Border perennial

M. betonicifolia

You will find numerous species offered in specialist catalogues but you are only likely to find two at the garden centre. They need moisture-retentive and lime-free soil.

VARIETIES

M. betonicifolia – 90 cm. Sky blue. Himalayan Poppy. June-July. 8 cm wide flowers. Difficult in most gardens. Provide some shade, moisture in summer and perhaps protection against winter rain.

M. cambrica – 30 cm. Yellow or orange. Welsh Poppy. June-September. Much easier to grow.

FLOWER TIME
Depends on species

TOP TIPS
Short lived, so divide clumps after flowering to replenish stock.

MESEMBRYANTHEMUM

M. occulatus 'Lunette'
Livingstone Daisy

Bedding plant: half-hardy annual

M. criniflorum

The ground-hugging stems bear glistening succulent leaves and daisy-like flowers in a wide array of colours. Unfortunately the blooms open only when the sun is shining.

VARIETIES

M. criniflorum – 10-15 cm. Various. The basic species — usually sold as a mixture. Sometimes bicoloured with a pale-coloured central zone.

M. occulatus 'Lunette' – 15 cm. Yellow. The one to grow for single-coloured flowers — there is a central red disc. Less inclined to close than M. criniflorum.

FLOWER TIME
July — September

TOP TIPS
Grow something else if the site is shady or clayey.

MIMULUS

M. 'Calypso Mixed'
Annual Monkey Flower

Bedding plant: half-hardy annual

M. hybridus

Not many annuals will bloom abundantly in a shady spot. Busy Lizzie or Bedding Begonia is the usual choice, but you can plant a Mimulus hybrid for a bright display.

VARIETIES

The modern varieties of **M. hybridus** are better than the older ones.

M. 'Malibu' – 15 cm. Various.

M. 'Magic' – 15 cm. Various. Buy single colours or a mixture.

M. 'Calypso' – 25 cm. Various. The widest range of colours.

M. 'Viva' – 30 cm. Red-blotched yellow. The tallest and showiest.

FLOWER TIME
June — September

TOP TIPS
A moisture-loving plant — water copiously in dry weather.

MIMULUS

Perennial Monkey Flower

Border perennial
Rockery perennial
Bog plant

M. burnetii

SITE & SOIL
15

PROPAGATION
6

Perennial types of Mimulus are less popular than the annual ones. All require moist soil and some shade, but the places suited to the various species differ widely.

VARIETIES

M.cardinalis – 90 cm. Red. Good border variety.
There are several rockery types:
M.burnetii – 10 cm. Copper/yellow.
M.'Whitecroft Scarlet' – 10 cm.
M.'Andean Nymph' – 20 cm. Cream/pink. Not reliably hardy.
There are wet ground varieties:
M.guttatus – 30 cm. Yellow.

FLOWER TIME
June — September

TOP TIPS
Not all are fully hardy — check the label before buying.

MINA

Spanish Flag

Bedding plant:
half-hardy annual

M. lobata

SITE & SOIL
2

PROPAGATION
7

The flowers of the popular species change colour as they age. The twining stems will clothe a trellis or fence and in summer banana-shaped blooms appear.

VARIETIES

M.lobata (Ipomoea lobata) – 1.5 m. First flowers red, changing to orange and yellow and finally white. Listed in many seed catalogues and is available in pots at some garden centres in spring.
M.pennata – 1.5 m. Red. Quite different to M. lobata — star-shaped flowers do not change colour.

FLOWER TIME
July — October

TOP TIPS
Grow it as a change from usual annual climbers such as Nasturtium.

MONARDA

Bergamot

Border perennial

M. 'Croftway Pink'

SITE & SOIL
13

PROPAGATION
2

The flower-heads, made up of whorls of flowers, are borne on top of stiff stems. Divide and replant every three years to keep the plants vigorous — cut back the stems in autumn.

VARIETIES

M.didyma – 90 cm. Pink or red. Numerous hybrids are available:
M.'Cambridge Scarlet' – 75 cm. Red.
M.'Croftway Pink' – 75 cm. Pink.
M.'Fishes' – 70 cm. Pink.
M.'Prairie Night' – 90 cm. Purple.
M.'Schneewitchen' – 90 cm. White.
M.'Capricorn' – 90 cm. Red-purple.

FLOWER TIME
June — September

TOP TIPS
Add compost before planting. Water in dry weather.

MUSCARI
Bulb

M. botryoides 'Album'

M. armeniacum 'Blue Spike'

Grape Hyacinth

Nobody sings its praises because it has none of the glamour of the showier spring bulbs — tiny bell- or flask-shaped flowers are clustered on leafless stems.

VARIETIES

M. armeniacum – 20 cm. White-edged blue. April-May. Leaves appear in autumn.
M. a. 'Blue Spike' – 15 cm. Blue. Double.
M. azureum – 10 cm. Dark-striped blue. March.
M. botryoides 'Album' – 15 cm. White. April.

SITE & SOIL
2

PROPAGATION
20

FLOWER TIME
Depends on species

TOP TIPS
Looks best when massed as ground cover between taller spring flowers.

MYOSOTIS
Bedding plant: hardy biennial

M. sylvatica 'Ultramarine'

M. sylvatica 'Royal Blue'

Forget-me-not

The traditional ground cover for planting between tulips or wallflowers. Dwarf varieties are used here — there are taller ones for the border. Blue is the usual colour.

VARIETIES

M. sylvatica – 15-30 cm. Yellow-eyed blue flowers.
M. s. 'Blue Ball' – 15 cm. Blue.
M. s. 'Ultramarine' – 15 cm. Dark blue.
M. s. 'Victoria Rose' – 10 cm. Pink.
M. s. 'White Ball' – 15 cm. White.
M. s. 'Blue Basket' – 30 cm. Blue.
M. s. 'Royal Blue' – 30 cm. Blue.

SITE & SOIL
10

PROPAGATION
16

FLOWER TIME
April — May

TOP TIPS
Can be left as a perennial, but it soon deteriorates. Water in dry weather.

NARCISSUS
Bulb

N. 'Mount Hood'

Trumpet Daffodil

The common name 'Daffodil' is usually restricted to those varieties with a trumpet which is as long or longer than the petals. For cultural notes see Narcissus on page 77.

VARIETIES

Height 15-45 cm.
N. 'King Alfred' was once dominant, but now the name is used for other large yellows.
N. 'Golden Harvest' – Yellow.
N. 'Mount Hood' – White.
N. 'Magnet' – White/yellow.
N. 'Topolino' – White/yellow. 15 cm dwarf.

N. 'Golden Harvest'

SITE & SOIL
3

PROPAGATION
17

FLOWER TIME
March — April

TOP TIPS
Let the foliage die down naturally — do not tie in knots.

NARCISSUS

N. 'Professor Einstein'
Large-cupped Narcissus

Bulb

Varieties with a trumpet or cup which is shorter than the petals are usually referred to as Narcissi rather than Daffodils. For cultural notes see below.

N. 'Yellow Sun'

VARIETIES

Cup more than one-third of petal length. Height 30-60 cm.

N. 'Carlton' – Yellow. Large and popular.
N. 'Yellow Sun' – Yellow.
N. 'Desdemona' – White.
N. 'Professor Einstein' – White/orange. Very early.
N. 'Salome' – White/pink.

FLOWER TIME
March — April

TOP TIPS
Let the foliage die down naturally — do not tie in knots.

NARCISSUS

Narcissus

Bulb

N. 'Edward Buxton'

N. 'Thalia'

N. 'February Gold'

Included here are all the varieties apart from the large-cupped types of Narcissi and Daffodils described previously. There is a surprisingly large range of shapes, sizes and colours among the many hundreds of varieties which are available. All those listed are fully hardy and can be left to spread into clumps. Choose carefully — look for firm bulbs. Plant in August-October as soon as possible after buying — put coarse sand at the bottom of the hole and cover with soil to twice the height of the bulb.

VARIETIES

Small-cupped Narcissi – Cup less than one-third of petal length. Example: **N. 'Edward Buxton'**.
Double Narcissi – More than one ring of petals. Example: **N. 'Texas'**.
Triandrus Narcissi – More than one drooping flower per stem. Example: **N. 'Thalia'**.
Cyclamineus Narcissi – One drooping flower per stem. Small. Example: **N. 'February Gold'**.
Jonquilla Narcissi – More than one flower per stem. Broad petals. Example: **N. 'Pipit'**.
Poeticus Narcissi – White petals, red-edged cup. Example: **N. 'Actaea'**.
Wild Narcissi – The natural forms. Example: **N. bulbocodium**.

N. 'Texas'

N. bulbocodium

FLOWER TIME
March — April

TOP TIPS
Plant 10-20 cm apart. Let the foliage die down naturally — do not tie in knots. With naturalised bulbs do not cut the grass for a month after the flowers have faded.

NEMESIA

Bedding plant: half-hardy annual

N. strumosa

SITE & SOIL
3

PROPAGATION
7

N. strumosa 'Carnival Mixed'

Nemesia

A mixture provides self-colours, bicolours and tricolours. The time between sowing and flowering is short, but flowering ends quickly in hot summers.

VARIETIES

N. strumosa – 15-25 cm. Various. 3 cm wide lipped flowers.
N. s. 'Fire King' – 20 cm. Red.
N. s. 'Blue Gem' – 20 cm. Blue.
N. s. 'KLM' – 20 cm. Blue/white.
N. s. 'Carnival Mixed' – 20 cm. Various. Large flowers.
N. s. 'Sundrops Mixed' – 15 cm. Various. Compact.

FLOWER TIME
June — September

TOP TIPS
Pinch out tips after bedding out — cut back after first flush.

NEMOPHILA

Hardy annual

N. menziesii

SITE & SOIL
13

PROPAGATION
21

N. maculata

Nemophila

A low-growing carpeter for the border edge or rockery. The buttercup-shaped flowers are borne above feathery leaves from early summer to the first frosts.

VARIETIES

N. menziesii – 20 cm. White-eyed blue. Baby Blue Eyes. 4 cm wide flowers — good ground cover for a humus-rich partly shaded bed, rockery or border.
N. maculata – 15 cm. Violet-spotted white. Five Spot. 2 cm wide flowers — attractive but harder to find than N. menziesii.

FLOWER TIME
June — October

TOP TIPS
Dig in organic matter before planting. Water copiously in dry weather.

NEPETA

Border perennial

N. mussinii

SITE & SOIL
2

PROPAGATION
6

N. 'Six Hills Giant'

Catmint

A popular ground cover with aromatic foliage and spikes of small flowers. It will flourish in poor soil but good drainage is essential. Dead-head faded blooms.

VARIETIES

N. mussinii – 30 cm. Lavender. 1 cm long tubular flowers.
N. m. 'Little Titch' – 15 cm. Mauve.
N. nervosa – 50 cm. Violet-blue.
N. 'Souvenir d'Andre Chaudron' – 45 cm. Blue-purple. Large flowers.
N. 'Six Hills Giant' – 90 cm. Lavender. Vigorous.
N. govaniana – 90 cm. Yellow.

FLOWER TIME
May — September

TOP TIPS
Remove old growth when new shoots appear in spring.

NICOTIANA

N. 'Sensation Mixed'
Tobacco Plant

Bedding plant:
half-hardy annual

The old-fashioned N. alata has a strong fragrance but it needs staking and the flowers close during the day. Nowadays there are dwarf hybrids which are open all day.

VARIETIES

N. alata – 90 cm. Yellow.
N. 'Domino Mixed' – 30 cm. Various. The most popular dwarf.
N. 'Heaven Scent' – 60 cm. Various. A modern fragrant variety.
N. 'Lime Green' – 60 cm. Pale green.
N. 'Sensation Mixed' – 90 cm. Various.

N. 'Lime Green'

SITE & SOIL
3

PROPAGATION
7

FLOWER TIME
June — October

TOP TIPS
If fragrance is important look for N. 'Heaven Scent'.

NIGELLA

N. damascena 'Persian Jewels'
Love-in-a-mist

Hardy annual

The blue ones have been grown for generations but multicoloured mixtures are now more popular. Easy to grow, but the flowering season is short.

VARIETIES

N. damascena – 45 cm. Blue.
N. d. 'Miss Jekyll' – 45 cm. Blue. The favourite blue variety.
N. d. 'Blue Midget' – 20 cm. Blue.
N. d. 'Persian Pink' – 45 cm. Pink.
N. d. 'Persian Jewels' – 45 cm. Various. The most popular mixture.
N. d. orientalis 'Transformer' – 40 cm. Yellow.

N. damascena 'Miss Jekyll'

SITE & SOIL
3

PROPAGATION
21

FLOWER TIME
June — August

TOP TIPS
Dig in compost before sowing. Dead-head spent blooms.

NOLANA

N. paradoxa 'Blue Bird'
Chilean Bellflower

Bedding plant:
half-hardy annual

Appeared in the 1980s as a trumpet-flowered alternative to Petunia. The 5 cm wide frilly-edged blooms are impressive and cover the foliage from early summer to autumn.

VARIETIES

N. paradoxa 'Blue Bird' – 25 cm. Yellow-centred, white-throated blue.
N. p. 'Snow Bird' – 30 cm. Yellow-centred white. Similar growth habit to N. p. 'Blue Bird'.
N. p. 'Shooting Star' – 40 cm. Pale blue. Semi-trailing growth habit — use it for ground cover or in hanging baskets.

N. paradoxa 'Blue Bird'

SITE & SOIL
1

PROPAGATION
7

FLOWER TIME
June — October

TOP TIPS
A sun-lover — choose something else if the site is shady.

OENOTHERA

O. fruticosa 'Fireworks'

Evening Primrose

Border perennial

Some but not all are night-flowering and despite the common name the flowers are poppy- and not primrose-like. They need non-heavy soil and lots of sun.

O. macrocarpa

VARIETIES

O. macrocarpa – 15 cm. Yellow. Dwarf. Bears the largest flowers.
O. fruticosa 'Fireworks' – 60 cm. Yellow. Red buds. Purple-green leaves.
O. glauca 'Erica Robin' – 30 cm. Yellow. Pink-green foliage.
O. speciosa 'Siskiyou' – 15 cm. Pink.

SITE & SOIL
18

PROPAGATION
6

FLOWER TIME
July — September

TOP TIPS
Mulch in spring — water in dry weather. Cut down in late autumn.

OMPHALODES

O. verna

Omphalodes

Border perennial
Rockery perennial

A useful plant with loose sprays of forget me not-like flowers for growing under shrubs or trees in water-retentive soil. The pointed leaves are evergreen.

O. cappodocica 'Anthea Bloom'

VARIETIES

O. verna – 15 cm. White-eyed blue. Blue-eyed Mary.
O. v. 'Alba' – 15 cm. White.
O. cappodocica – 30 cm. Blue. Smaller flowers than O. verna.
O. c. 'Anthea Bloom' – 30 cm. Sky blue.
O. c. 'Starry Eyes' – 30 cm. Blue-striped white.

SITE & SOIL
15

PROPAGATION
1

FLOWER TIME
March — May

TOP TIPS
Dig in compost before planting — mulch around the stems in spring.

ORNITHOGALUM

O. umbellatum

Ornithogalum

Bulb

There are two groups. The tender ones are planted in April for summer flowers after which they are discarded. The hardy ones are grown in the rock garden or grassland.

O. thyrsoides

VARIETIES

O. thyrsoides – 45 cm. White. July-August. Chincherinchee. Best known tender species. Flowers are clustered on a conical spike.
O. nutans – 45 cm. Green-backed white. April-May. Pendent blooms.
O. umbellatum – 30 cm. White. April-May. Star of Bethlehem. Blooms face upwards.

SITE & SOIL
4

PROPAGATION
20

FLOWER TIME
Depends on species

TOP TIPS
The hardy species deserve to be more widely grown.

OSTEOSPERMUM

O. 'Whirligig'

Osteospermum

Bedding plant:
half-hardy annual
Border perennial

O. 'Starshine'

Once a rarity — now on offer at every garden centre. Some have blooms in the standard daisy pattern but the most eye-catching ones have spoon-shaped petals.

VARIETIES

Many hybrids are sold as bedding plants – 30-60 cm. Various. 5-8 cm wide flowers:
O. 'Whirligig' – Blue-backed white. Spoon-petalled.
O. 'Starshine' – Pink. Compact.
O. 'Buttermilk' – Yellow.
There is one hardy species:
O. jucundum – 30 cm. Pink.

SITE & SOIL
1

PROPAGATION
7

FLOWER TIME
June — October

TOP TIPS
Quite fussy — good drainage, some shelter and no shade are necessary.

OXALIS

O. laciniata

Oxalis

Rockery perennial

O. adenophylla

The five-petalled flowers open when the sun shines — the clover-like leaves below may be flat or folded. Easy to grow — dig in peat or compost before planting.

VARIETIES

O. adenophylla – 8 cm. Silvery-pink. Grey-green pleated leaves. The most popular species.
O. enneaphylla – 8 cm. White, pink or red. Restrained growth habit.
O. laciniata – 8 cm. Blue.
O. 'Ione Hecker' – 8 cm. Dark-veined purple. Non-invasive.
O. deppei – 20 cm. Pink.

SITE & SOIL
1

PROPAGATION
1

FLOWER TIME
June — July

TOP TIPS
Make sure you choose a hardy non-invasive variety for the rockery.

PAEONIA

P. lactiflora
'Bowl of Beauty'

Peony

Border perennial

P. officinalis
'Rosea Plena'

Large-headed beauties for the border. Have patience — new plants may take several years to establish. Dig in compost before planting, stake stems and water in dry weather.

VARIETIES

P. officinalis – 60 cm. Various. May-June. Common Peony. **P.o. 'Rosea Plena'** (Pink. Double).
P. lactiflora – 75-90 cm. Various. June-July. Chinese Peony.
P.l. 'Bowl of Beauty' (Cream/pink).
P.l. 'Sarah Bernhardt' (Pink).
P. mlokosewitschii – 45 cm. Yellow. April-May. April-flowering Peony.

SITE & SOIL
3

PROPAGATION
13

FLOWER TIME
Depends on species

TOP TIPS
Do not dig up and divide clumps to increase your stock.

PAPAVER

P. orientale 'Goliath'
Oriental Poppy

Border perennial

P. orientale 'Mrs. Perry'

SITE & SOIL
2

PROPAGATION
1

The Oriental Poppy is a fine sight when in full bloom, but the flowers are short-lived and the foliage looks untidy when the flowering season is over. Divide every three years.

VARIETIES

P. orientale – 45-90 cm. Various. 10-15 cm wide bowl-shaped blooms. Black-based petals, black anthers. Many varieties available:
P. o. 'Mrs. Perry' – Salmon-pink.
P. o. 'Goliath' – Red.
P. o. 'Picotee' – Orange-edged white.
P. o. 'Marcus Perry' – Vermilion.
P. o. 'May Sadler' – Salmon-pink.

FLOWER TIME
May — July

TOP TIPS
Cut down leaves and flower stalks when blooms have faded.

PAPAVER

P. nudicaule
Annual Poppy

Hardy annual
Hardy biennial

P. somniferum

SITE & SOIL
2

PROPAGATION
9/16

Dainty-looking plants — buds bow their heads, petals flutter in the breeze and the flowers are short-lived. Despite appearances they are tough and do not need staking.

VARIETIES

P. rhoeas – Most popular species:
P. r. 'Shirley Mixed' – 60 cm. Various.
P. commutatum 'Ladybird' – 30 cm. Black-blotched red.
P. somniferum – 1.2 m. Various. Double. Opium Poppy.
P. nudicaule – 60 cm. Various. Iceland Poppy. Grow as a biennial.

FLOWER TIME
June — September

TOP TIPS
Dead-heading is necessary to prolong the flowering season.

PELARGONIUM

P. 'Crocodile'
Ivy-leaved Geranium

Bedding plant: tender perennial

P. peltatum hybrid

SITE & SOIL
3

PROPAGATION
11/25

This relative of the Bedding Geranium bears fleshy leaves on trailing stems in hanging baskets and tubs. Flowers are 1-2.5 cm across. For cultural notes see page 83.

VARIETIES

P. peltatum – 30-90 cm. White, pink, red or mauve. Ivy-shaped leaves. Numerous hybrids are available:
P. 'L'Elegante' – Pink. White-edged green leaves.
P. 'La France' – Mauve.
P. 'Crocodile' – Pink. Cream-netted green leaves.
P. 'Summer Showers' – Various.

FLOWER TIME
June — October

TOP TIPS
Buy as plugs and grow on where a large number is required.

PELARGONIUM Bedding Geranium

Bedding plant: tender perennial

P. hortorum hybrid

Single flower

Double flower

Call them Bedding or Zonal Geraniums — these are the varieties of Pelargonium you see bedded out everywhere in summer. There are 60 cm giants and 15 cm dwarfs with heads of 1-2.5 cm wide flowers. Geraniums can withstand dry conditions better than most plants. Constant watering is an easy way to kill them, so water only if dry weather is prolonged. Lift and pot up the plants before the frosts arrive. Keep cool over winter — water only if the leaves start to flag. Increase watering in spring.

P. 'Red Elite'

VARIETIES

P. hortorum – 15-60 cm. Rounded leaves. Many hybrids are available. Some are raised from cuttings:
Standard varieties – **P. 'Paul Crampel'**.
Deacon varieties (masses of small flower-heads) – **P. 'Deacon Bonanza'**.
Irene varieties (semi-double flowers) – **P. 'Electra'**.
Cactus varieties (narrow petals) – **P. 'Noel'**.
Miniature varieties – **P. 'Fantasia'**.
Other varieties are raised from seed – **P. 'Red Elite'**, **P. 'Century'** (large flower-heads), **P. 'Multibloom'** (many flower-heads), **P. 'Breakaway'** (spreading stems).

P. 'Multibloom Mixed'

FLOWER TIME
June — October

TOP TIPS
Water the pots a few hours before planting — make sure the plants have been properly hardened off. Pinch out tips occasionally. Dead-head spent blooms.

Cactus flower

SITE & SOIL
3

PROPAGATION
11/25

PELARGONIUM Regal Pelargonium

P. 'Carisbrooke'

Bedding plant: tender perennial

P. domesticum hybrid

SITE & SOIL
3

PROPAGATION
11

This showy but rather tender relative of the Bedding Geranium bears large flowers which are usually marked with a darker colour and ruffled. For cultural notes see above.

VARIETIES

P. domesticum – 30-60 cm. Various. Saw-edged leaves. Numerous hybrids are available:
P. 'Carisbrooke' – Pink/red.
P. 'Aztec' – White/pink.
P. 'Elsie Hickman' – White/pink/red.
P. 'Lavender Grand Slam' – Mauve/purple.
P. 'Purple Emperor' – Mauve/red.

FLOWER TIME
June — October

TOP TIPS
Not suitable for cold or exposed sites — grow Bedding Geraniums.

PENSTEMON

P. 'Garnet'

Penstemon

Border perennial
Rockery perennial
Bedding plant:
half-hardy annual

P. 'Evelyn'

Once considered quite tender, but it seems that winter death is usually due to rotting rather than freezing of the crown. Some varieties can be grown from seed as annuals.

VARIETIES

P. 'Evelyn' – 60 cm. Pink.
P. 'Garnet' – 80 cm. Dark red. Bushy. One of the hardiest.
P. 'Hidcote Pink' – 70 cm. Pink.
P. 'Countess of Dalkeith' – 1 m. White-throated purple.
P. newberryi – 25 cm. Dark pink.
P. 'Hyacinth-flowered Mixture' – 45 cm. Various. Sold as seed.

FLOWER TIME
July — October

TOP TIPS
Cover crowns in winter. Dead-head faded summer blooms.

PETUNIA

Petunia

Bedding plant:
half-hardy annual

P. hybrida
Grandiflora group

P. hybrida
Milliflora group

P. 'Frenzy Mixed'

Now one of the most popular of all bedding plants — the spreading and trailing types are the favourite subjects for tubs, window boxes and hanging baskets. The range these days is extensive — there are upright, spreading and trailing ones, singles and doubles, self-coloured and multicoloured varieties and petals with smooth or ruffled edges. Starting from seed is possible but difficult — buy small seedlings or plugs and grow on. The floral display may disappoint in a cool and wet summer.

VARIETIES

There are 4 groups of **P. hybrida**.
The Multiflora group contains the most popular bedding varieties – 15-45 cm. 5 cm wide flowers — more rain-resistant than larger-flowered ones. Examples: **P. 'Resisto Mixed'**, **P. 'Frenzy Mixed'**. Doubles include **P. 'Duo Mixed'**.
The Grandiflora group has larger flowers – 10-15 cm across. Examples: **P. 'Lavender Storm'**.
The Milliflora group has masses of 2 cm flowers. Examples: **P. 'Fantasy'**, **P. 'Million Bells'**.
The Surfinia group are true trailers – 1.2 m. Rooted cuttings (not seeds) available. Examples: **P. 'Hot Pink'**, **P. 'Blue Vein'**.

P. hybrida
Surfinia group

P. 'Million Bells'

FLOWER TIME
June — October

TOP TIPS
Buy plants which are not in flower and pinch out the tips when the stems are 10-15 cm high. Cut back straggly shoots to maintain bushy habit. Dead-head regularly.

PHACELIA

Hardy annual

P. campanularia

P. 'Blue Bonnet'

Phacelia

The outstanding feature of this annual is the intense blue of the flower. The upturned bells above the greyish foliage have gentian-coloured petals and bright yellow stamens.

VARIETIES

P. campanularia – 25 cm. Blue. Californian Bluebell. 3 cm wide flowers. The most popular type.

P. 'Blue Bonnet' – 50 cm. Blue. Bright flowers like above.

P. viscida – 45 cm. Blue. Flowers borne on long spikes.

P. tanacetifolia – 75 cm. Lavender. Flowers borne on curved spikes.

FLOWER TIME
June — September

TOP TIPS
Resents transplanting — sow directly in the bed and thin as required.

PHLOX

Border perennial
Rockery perennial

P. paniculata

SITE & SOIL

13

PROPAGATION

2

P. maculata

Border Phlox

The sheets of colour in late summer are one of the mainstays of the border — there are also several dwarfs for the rockery. Mulch in spring and stake if necessary.

VARIETIES

P. paniculata – 80 cm. Various. July-September. Flowers in rounded clusters.

P. p. 'White Admiral' – White.

P. p. 'Starfire' – Red.

P. maculata – 80 cm. Various. July-September. Flowers in columns.

P. subulata – 8 cm. Various. April-May. Moss Phlox for the rockery.

FLOWER TIME
Depends on species

TOP TIPS
Dig in compost before planting — cut down in late autumn.

PHLOX

Bedding plant:
half-hardy annual

P. drummondii

SITE & SOIL

13

PROPAGATION

7

P. drummondii
'Tapestry Mixed'

Annual Phlox

The 10 cm wide flower-heads bear blooms which may be smooth-edged or distinctly star-like. Once tall and untidy — nowadays colourful dwarfs are more popular.

VARIETIES

P. drummondii is the basic species. Many varieties are available:

P. d. 'Tapestry Mixed' – 50 cm. A modern multicoloured tall variety.

P. d. 'Star Twinkles' – 20 cm. Star-shaped flowers. Various.

P. d. 'Beauty Mixed' – 20 cm. Large flowers in many colours.

P. d. 'African Sunset' – 15 cm. Red.

FLOWER TIME
July — September

TOP TIPS
Sow outdoors in April in mild areas. Do not over-water.

PHYSALIS

Border perennial

P. alkekengi 'Franchetii'

P. alkekengi 'Franchetii'
Chinese Lantern

A plant for the flower arranger. The small white blooms have little decorative value, but the picture changes when lantern-like structures form around the fruits.

VARIETIES

P. alkekengi – 60 cm. Orange lanterns.
P. a. 'Franchetii' – 60 cm. Orange-red lanterns. The only Chinese Lantern you are likely to find. Fruiting period September-October. 5 cm long inflated calyces (lanterns). Cut stems, tie in bunches and hang upside-down to dry.

FLOWER TIME
July — August

TOP TIPS
Spreads by creeping underground stems so can be invasive.

PHYSOSTEGIA

Border perennial

P. virginiana 'Vivid'

SITE & SOIL
4

PROPAGATION
6

P. virginiana 'Summer Snow'
Obedience Plant

Move the tubular flowers on the upright spikes and they will stay in the new position — hence the common name. An easy plant to grow, but tall varieties may need staking.

VARIETIES

P. virginiana – 60 cm-1.2 m. White, pink or purple. The only species you are likely to find. 3 cm long flowers are borne in vertical rows on each spike.
P. v. 'Vivid' – 60 cm. Pink.
P. v. 'Summer Snow' – 60 cm. White.
P. v. 'Bouquet Rose' – 1.2 m. Lilac.

FLOWER TIME
July — September

TOP TIPS
Dig in compost before planting — water in dry weather.

PLATYCODON

Border perennial

P. grandiflorus 'Mariesii'

SITE & SOIL
3

PROPAGATION
7

P. grandiflorus 'Mariesii'
Balloon Flower

An unusual and attractive border plant — the buds swell into large angular balloons before opening into star-faced flowers. All top-growth disappears in winter.

VARIETIES

P. grandiflorus – 60 cm. Purple. 5 cm wide flowers. Dislikes root disturbance. The only garden species.
P. g. 'Mariesii' – 30 cm. Blue. The favourite variety.
P. g. 'Albus' – 60 cm. White.
P. g. 'Fuji Pink' – 60 cm. Pink.
P. g. 'Mother of Pearl' – 60 cm. Pink.

FLOWER TIME
June — September

TOP TIPS
Mulch around the stems in early summer and cut back in autumn.

POLEMONIUM

P. foliosissimum
Jacob's Ladder

Border perennial

P. caeruleum

The leaves are divided into a series of rung-like leaflets — hence the common name. An easy plant to grow but it is not long-lived. Dead-head to prolong the flowering season.

VARIETIES

P. caeruleum – 60 cm. Blue. The most popular species:
P. c. 'Album' – 60 cm. White.
P. c. 'Brise d'Anjou' – 60 cm. Mauve. Grown for its yellow-edged green leaves.
P. foliosissimum – 90 cm. Violet, yellow or white.
P. reptans – 30 cm. Lilac.

SITE & SOIL
6

PROPAGATION
2

FLOWER TIME
June — August

TOP TIPS
Dig in compost before planting. Cut down stems in autumn.

POLYGONATUM

P. hybridum
Solomon's Seal

Border perennial
Rockery perennial

P. hybridum

A shade-lover which will thrive in the deep shadow of trees and shrubs. The leaves clasp the arching stems which bear pendent bell-like flowers in early summer.

VARIETIES

P. hybridum – 1 m. Green-tipped white. The most popular species.
P. h. 'Striatum' – 60 cm. Green-tipped white. Cream-striped green leaves.
P. hookeri – 10 cm. Lilac. Unusual dwarf with erect flowers.
P. odoratum – 1 m. White.
P. humile – 20 cm. White.

SITE & SOIL
20

PROPAGATION
2

FLOWER TIME
May — June

TOP TIPS
Add compost before planting, mulch in spring and water in dry weather.

POLYGONUM

P. bistorta 'Superbum'
Knotweed

Border perennial
Rockery perennial
Bog plant

P. affine 'Donald Lowndes'

There are varieties for the border, poolside and rockery — the tiny flowers are borne on upright spikes and most are vigorous ground covers. Often listed as Persicaria.

VARIETIES

P. (Persicaria) affine – 30 cm. Pink. July-September. The best-known.
P. a. 'Donald Lowndes' – Salmon.
P. amplexicaule 'Firetail' – 90 cm. Red. June-September.
P. bistorta 'Superbum' – 90 cm. Pink. July-September. Bog garden.
P. vaccinifolium – 10 cm. Pink. September-November. Rockery.

SITE & SOIL
13

PROPAGATION
2

FLOWER TIME
Depends on species

TOP TIPS
Most but not all are invasive, so choose and plant with care.

PORTULACA

Bedding plant: half-hardy annual

P. grandiflora
'Double Mixed'

Sun Plant

This ground-hugging wide-spreading succulent provides summer-long colour if the conditions are right. The flowers are often ruffled and the petals have a satin-like sheen.

P. grandiflora

VARIETIES

P. grandiflora – 15 cm. Various. 3 cm wide flowers. Most varieties close their flowers in dull weather.
P. g. 'Double Mixed' – 15 cm. Various. Rose-like blooms.
P. g. 'Sundance' – 15 cm. Various. 5 cm wide flowers. Semi-trailing.
P. g. 'Sundial' – 10 cm. Various. Best variety in poor weather.

SITE & SOIL
18

PROPAGATION
7

FLOWER TIME
June — September

TOP TIPS
Sandy soil and a site free from any shade are essential.

POTENTILLA

Border perennial

P. 'William Rollison'

Cinquefoil

Border Potentillas are not as popular as the shrubby types — both have small leaves with bright flowers but the border varieties have weak sprawling stems and not woody ones.

P. 'Gibson's Scarlet'

VARIETIES

Several hybrids are available:
P. 'William Rollison' – 45 cm. Orange/yellow. Semi-double.
P. 'Gibson's Scarlet' – 30 cm. Red.
P. 'Etna' – 45 cm. Dark red.
There are a few popular species:
P. nepalensis 'Miss Willmott' – 30 cm. Pink. Widely available.
P. tonguei – 20 cm. Apricot.

SITE & SOIL
2

PROPAGATION
2

FLOWER TIME
June — August

TOP TIPS
Water in dry weather and cut down the stems in autumn.

PRIMULA

Hardy perennial

P. vulgaris

Primrose/Polyanthus

The Common Primrose has a place in the garden and so have its low-growing hybrids. The taller and hardier hybrids of this Primrose and the Cowslip are known as Polyanthus.

P. variabilis

VARIETIES

P. vulgaris – 10 cm. Yellow. Common Primrose. Hybrids include:
P. 'Wanda' – 10 cm. Purple.
P. variabilis – 20-30 cm. Various. Polyanthus. Varieties include:
P. v. 'Pacific Giants' – Various. Largest flowers.
P. v. 'Crescendo' – Various. Maximum winter reliability.

SITE & SOIL
20

PROPAGATION
2

FLOWER TIME
March — May

TOP TIPS
Raising from seed is not easy — buy plants or divide clumps.

PRIMULA

Rockery perennial

P. auricula
'Old Yellow Dusty Miller'
Border Auricula

Great favourites in earlier times — fleshy leaves which are usually covered with a mealy deposit and flowers which usually bear several coloured rings.

VARIETIES

P. auricula – 15 cm. Various. Only a few of the vast range of Auriculas are reliable enough for growing outdoors. Examples include:

P. a. 'Old Yellow Dusty Miller' – Yellow.

P. a. 'McWatt's Blue' – Grey-blue.

P. a. 'Old Suffolk Bronze' – Red/brown/yellow.

SITE & SOIL
20

PROPAGATION
20

FLOWER TIME
March — April

TOP TIPS
Make sure the variety you buy is recommended for outdoors.

PRIMULA

Border perennial
Bog plant

P. denticulata
Border Primula

The taller hardy Primulas belong here — stems are 30-90 cm high and the leaves are 10-20 cm long. Some but not all need boggy ground. All tend to be short-lived.

P. japonica

VARIETIES

Candelabra Primroses – Flowers in whorls. **P. japonica** – 45 cm. Various. May-June. **P. bulleyana** – 70 cm. Yellow. June-July.

Drumstick Primroses – Flowers in globular heads. **P. denticulata** – 30 cm. Lilac. March-May.

Other types include **P. florindae** – 60 cm. Yellow. July-August.

SITE & SOIL
20

PROPAGATION
6

FLOWER TIME
Depends on species

TOP TIPS
Mulch in spring, water in summer and dead-head faded blooms.

PRIMULA

Rockery perennial

P. marginata
Rockery Primula

There are many dwarf Primulas which are suitable for the rock garden — flower stalks with upright or pendent blooms arise from leafy rosettes.

VARIETIES

P. marginata – 10 cm. Blue or lavender. April. Fragrant.

P. pubescens – 10 cm. Various. April-May.

P. p. 'Harlow Carr' – Cream.

P. p. 'Faldonside' – White-eyed pink.

P. p. 'Mrs. Wilson' – White-eyed pink.

P. minima – 5 cm. Various. May.

SITE & SOIL
20

PROPAGATION
20

FLOWER TIME
Depends on species

TOP TIPS
Check the site and cultural requirements before making your choice.

PRUNELLA

P. grandiflora

Self-heal

Border perennial
Rockery perennial

P. grandiflora

A mat-forming evergreen for growing between shrubs or covering bare spaces in the rockery. Not often seen, but it is useful for keeping down weeds. Water in dry weather.

VARIETIES

P. grandiflora – 25 cm. Dark-lipped pale purple. Large Self-heal. This is the species to buy rather than the wild flower **P. vulgaris**. Look for one of its varieties:
P. g. 'Loveliness' – Mauve.
P. g. 'Pink Loveliness' – Pink.
P. g. 'White Loveliness' – White.
P. g. 'Rosea' – Rose-pink.

SITE & SOIL
5

PROPAGATION
2

FLOWER TIME
June — August

TOP TIPS
Can be invasive — lift, divide and replant every three years.

PULMONARIA

P. saccharata

Lungwort

Border perennial

P. angustifolia

The old-fashioned Lungwort has white-spotted leaves and flowers which change from pink to blue, but you will also find all-green types with flowers in a range of colours.

VARIETIES

P. officinalis – 30 cm. Blue. Silver-splashed leaves. Spreads rapidly.
P. o. 'Sissinghurst White' – White.
P. saccharata – 30 cm. Various.
P. s. 'Mrs. Moon' – Pink.
P. s. 'Argentea' – Violet.
P. rubra 'Redstart' – 40 cm. Red.
P. angustifolia – 30 cm. Blue. All-green leaves.

SITE & SOIL
20

PROPAGATION
2

FLOWER TIME
April — May

TOP TIPS
Can be invasive — lift, divide and replant every three years.

PULSATILLA

P. vulgaris

Pasque Flower

Rockery perennial

P. vernalis

In spring the flower stems emerge, crowned with silky buds. These buds open into starry flowers. Next the ferny leaves appear and then there are attractive seed heads.

VARIETIES

P. vulgaris – 25 cm. Gold-centred pale purple.
P. v. 'Alba' – White.
P. v. 'Barton's Pink' – Pink.
P. v. 'Rubra' – Red.
P. vernalis – 25 cm. Purple-flushed white. Needs winter protection.
P. alpina 'Apiifolia' – 25 cm. Yellow. Bell-shaped flowers.

SITE & SOIL
2

PROPAGATION
13

FLOWER TIME
April — May

TOP TIPS
Dislikes root disturbance — do not lift and divide. Plant firmly.

PUSCHKINIA

Bulb

P. scilloides

SITE & SOIL
3

PROPAGATION
17

P. scilloides 'Alba'
Striped Squill

A hardy and trouble-free bulb. Attractive starry flowers appear early in the year and it increases to form large clumps, yet it remains a poor relation of the bluebells.

VARIETIES

P. scilloides (P. libanica) – 10 cm. Silvery blue. Each stem carries 6-12 flowers — each petal has a central dark blue stripe. Flowers are 1 cm across. Plant in groups for maximum effect — set bulbs 5 cm deep in September-October.

P. s. 'Alba' – White. Less eye-catching than the species.

FLOWER TIME
March — April

TOP TIPS
When dividing clumps replant at once. Add compost before planting.

RANUNCULUS

Bulb

R. asiaticus

SITE & SOIL
2

PROPAGATION
27

R. asiaticus 'Accolade Mixed'
Persian Buttercup

The showiest Ranunculus — bright semi-double or ball-shaped double blooms. Plant with claws down in March — lift in late summer and store over winter.

VARIETIES

R. asiaticus – 25-30 cm. Various. The basic species — flowers 8-12 cm across. Spring-planted bulbs bloom in July-August. Many types available, but nearly always bought as a mixture.

R. a. 'Accolade' – 25-30 cm. Various. Seed-raised strain available as plants in bloom in April-May.

FLOWER TIME
Depends on variety

TOP TIPS
Soak the bulbs in cold water for several hours before planting.

RANUNCULUS

Border perennial

R. acris 'Flore Pleno'

SITE & SOIL
13

PROPAGATION
2

R. aconitifolius 'Flore Pleno'
Border Buttercup

The Border Buttercups are taller than the Persian ones, but the flowers are smaller and less colourful. Bachelor's Buttons is an old favourite with masses of small flowers.

VARIETIES

R. aconitifolius – 60 cm. White. April-May. White Bachelor's Buttons. 3 cm wide single flowers.

R. a. 'Flore Pleno' – 90 cm. White. May-June. Double.

R. acris 'Flore Pleno' – 90 cm. Yellow. June-August. Yellow Bachelor's Buttons. 3 cm wide double flowers.

FLOWER TIME
Depends on species

TOP TIPS
Moist soil is necessary. The stems require some form of support.

RANUNCULUS

R. calandrinioides
Rockery Buttercup

Rockery perennial

There are numerous dwarf types which are suitable for the rock garden — some but not all are easy to grow. Choose with care — some are very invasive.

R. montanus 'Molten Gold'

VARIETIES

R. ficaria – 5-20 cm. Yellow. March-April. Lesser Celandine.
R. f. 'Brazen Hussy' – 10 cm. Yellow. Purple leaves.
R. f. 'Aurantiacus' – 10 cm. Orange.
R. montanus 'Molten Gold' – 10 cm. Yellow. March-April.
R. calandrinioides – 15 cm. Pink-flushed white. January.

SITE & SOIL
1

PROPAGATION
1

FLOWER TIME
Depends on variety

TOP TIPS
These dwarfs need full sun and hate poorly-drained soil.

RESEDA

R. odorata 'Giant'
Mignonette

Hardy annual

Nothing much to look at — the spreading stems are untidy and the clusters of tiny flowers are rather insipid. The strong fragrance, however, is outstanding.

R. odorata

VARIETIES

R. odorata – 30 cm. Greenish-yellow. Cone-like flower trusses. The only species you will find.
R. o. 'Machet' – Yellow/pink. The most popular variety.
R. o. 'Goliath' – Red.
R. o. 'Red Monarch' – Red/green.
R. o. 'Giant' – Pale green. Choose for maximum scent.

SITE & SOIL
17

PROPAGATION
21

FLOWER TIME
July — August

TOP TIPS
Disappointingly short flowering season in a hot and dry summer.

RHEUM

R. palmatum
Ornamental Rhubarb

Bog plant
Border perennial

A favourite plant for the poolside where it thrives in the boggy ground, but it can be grown in a humus-rich border. Plumes of tiny flowers appear on stout stems.

R. palmatum 'Atrosanguineum'

VARIETIES

R. palmatum – 1.8 m. Cream, green or red. Leaves purple-red below — spread 1.8 m or more.
R. p. 'Atrosanguineum' – 2 m. Red. Leaves purple-red when young.
R. p. 'Tanguticum' – 2 m. Red. Leaves are deeply divided.
R. 'Ace of Hearts' – 90 cm. Pale pink. Useful where space is limited.

SITE & SOIL
16

PROPAGATION
6

FLOWER TIME
May — June

TOP TIPS
Adequate space and copious watering in dry weather are essential.

RODGERSIA

Bog plant
Border perennial

R. aesculifolia

R. pinnata 'Superba'
Rodgersia

Like Rheum this bog garden plant can be grown in a moist border. Finger-like leaflets radiate from long stalks and petal-less flowers form fluffy heads.

VARIETIES

R. aesculifolia – 1.8 m. White. Horse chestnut-like bronzy leaves — spread 1.8 m or more.
R. pinnata 'Superba' – 1 m. Pink. Spread 1.2 m. The usual choice where space is limited.
R. podophylla – 1.5 m. Cream. More drought tolerant than the others, but display is disappointing.

SITE & SOIL
20

PROPAGATION
2

FLOWER TIME
July — August

TOP TIPS
Water copiously in dry weather and cut back in autumn.

RUDBECKIA

Border perennial

R. fulgida

R. fulgida 'Goldsturm'
Cone Flower

A popular provider of large yellow blooms in the border in late summer and autumn. The prominent cone-shaped disc at the centre of each flower is usually black or brown.

VARIETIES

R. fulgida – 60-90 cm. Yellow.
R. f. 'Goldsturm' – 60 cm. Yellow. Black cone. No need to stake.
R. 'Herbstsonne' – 1.8 m. Yellow. Green cone.
R. 'Goldquelle' – 90 cm. Yellow. Double.
R. occidentalis 'Green Wizard' – 1.2 m. Green. Black cone.

SITE & SOIL
3

PROPAGATION
2

FLOWER TIME
July — October

TOP TIPS
Stake stems to support tall varieties — cut down in late autumn.

RUDBECKIA

Bedding plant:
half-hardy annual

R. hirta 'Marmalade'

R. hirta 'Toto'
Annual Cone Flower

Daisy-like flowers in yellow, orange or mahogany red are carried on stout stems. In the centre of each flower is a prominent cone — the usual colour is brown or black.

VARIETIES

R. hirta is the basic species.
R. h. 'Gloriosa Daisy' – 80 cm. Yellow.
R. h. 'Marmalade' – 60 cm. Orange.
R. h. 'Goldilocks' – 50 cm. Yellow. Semi-double and double.
R. h. 'Toto' – 20 cm. Yellow.
R. h. 'Rustic Dwarfs' – 60 cm. Various.

SITE & SOIL
3

PROPAGATION
7

FLOWER TIME
July — October

TOP TIPS
Watch out for slugs. Provide support for tall varieties.

SALPIGLOSSIS

S. sinuata

Painted Tongue

Bedding plant: half-hardy annual

An exotic annual — the velvety, trumpet-shaped flowers are prominently veined. It is a demanding plant needing a sunny, sheltered site and loamy soil.

S. sinuata

VARIETIES

S. sinuata is the garden species.
S. s. 'Casino' – 45 cm. Various. Compact and more weather resistant than most.
S. s. 'Bolero' – 60 cm. Various.
S. s. 'Triumph' – 75 cm. Various.
S. s. 'Grandiflora' – 75 cm. Various. 5 cm wide flowers.
S. s. 'Festival' – 30 cm. Various.

SITE & SOIL
2

PROPAGATION
7

FLOWER TIME
July — September

TOP TIPS
Pinch out tips to promote bushiness. Support stems with twigs.

SALVIA

S. farinacea 'Strata'

Annual Sage

Bedding plant: half-hardy annual

The Scarlet Sage is a popular and inexpensive alternative to geraniums as a source of red in bedding schemes. There are other colours and other annual species of Salvia.

S. splendens

VARIETIES

S. splendens – 30 cm. Red. Scarlet Sage. 1 cm tubular flowers.
S. s. 'Blaze of Fire' – Red. Popular.
S. s. 'Dress Parade' – Various.
S. s. 'Salsa Mixture' – Various.
S. coccinea 'Coral Nymph' – 60 cm. Coral pink.
S. farinacea 'Strata' – 40 cm. White/blue.

SITE & SOIL
2

PROPAGATION
7

FLOWER TIME
June — October

TOP TIPS
Pinch out tips. Plant out when flowers have started to colour.

SALVIA

S. sylvestris 'May Night'

Border Sage

Border perennial

Hooded tubular flowers which are usually blue or lavender are borne on slender spikes. Attractive to bees and butterflies, but less popular than the annual Salvias.

S. nemorosa 'East Friesland'

VARIETIES

S. nemorosa 'East Friesland' – 45 cm. Blue-violet. July-August.
S. sylvestris 'May Night' – 75 cm. Blue-violet. May-June.
S. pratensis – 90 cm. Lavender. June-September. Meadow Clary.
S. patens – 60 cm. Dark blue. July-September. Gentian Sage.
S. p. 'Cambridge Blue' – Pale blue.

SITE & SOIL
3

PROPAGATION
2

FLOWER TIME
Depends on species

TOP TIPS
Stake taller varieties on exposed sites. Remove faded heads.

SAPONARIA

S. ocymoides
Soapwort

Rockery perennial
Border perennial

S. officinalis

The dwarf varieties will quickly carpet bare ground or cover stones in the rockery. The tall ones have erect stems which spread rapidly — not for the choice border.

VARIETIES

S. ocymoides – 10 cm. Pink. Wide-spreading. Popular.
S. 'Bressingham' – 10 cm. White-eyed pink. Non-invasive.
S. olivana – 5 cm. Pink. Neat compact cushion.
S. officinalis – 60 cm. Pink.
S. o. 'Rosea Plena' – 60 cm. Pink. Double.

SITE & SOIL
10

PROPAGATION
2

FLOWER TIME
July — September

TOP TIPS
Cut the stems of taller varieties down to ground level in autumn.

SAXIFRAGA

Saxifrage

Rockery perennial
Border perennial

S. urbium

A typical Saxifrage is a mossy mat or a group of leafy rosettes from which arises stalks bearing loose clusters of starry flowers in spring or early summer. Most are low-growing and ideal for the rockery, but a few are too tall and too invasive for the average rock garden. Outside these generalisations there are all sorts of variations. Some are evergreen and others are deciduous, some need full sun and others thrive in shade, some are easy and others are difficult — read the label before buying.

S. 'Peter Pan'

S. apiculata

VARIETIES

There are 4 groups:
The Border group consists of large and invasive types. Best-known example is **S. urbium** – 30 cm. Pink. May-July. London Pride.
The Encrusted group has rosettes of lime-encrusted leaves. May-July. Examples: **S. cochlearis** (20 cm. White), **S. 'Whitehill'** (15 cm. White).
The Mossy group forms moss-like hummocks. April-May. Examples: **S. 'Peter Pan'** (Pink), **S. 'Cloth of Gold'** (White. Gold leaves).
The Cushion group forms low mounds of lime-encrusted leaves. February-April. Example: **S. apiculata** (Yellow).

S. cochlearis

SITE & SOIL
12

PROPAGATION
32

FLOWER TIME
Depends on species

TOP TIPS
Provide a moist spot with some shade from the mid-day sun — only the Encrusted group thrives in full sun. Put gravel around low-growing types to keep soil off leaves.

SCABIOSA

S. stellata 'Paper Moon'
Sweet Scabious

Bedding plant: hardy annual

Annual varieties have never been popular like their perennial cousins. Modern types are available in many colours but much of the fragrance has gone.

S. atropurpurea

VARIETIES

S. atropurpurea – 45-75 cm. Various. 5 cm wide flower-heads.
S. a. 'Dwarf Double Mixed' – 45 cm.
S. a. 'Double Large-flowered Mixed' – 75 cm.
S. a. 'Blue Moon' – 60 cm. Blue.
S. stellata 'Paper Moon' – 90 cm. Lavender. Unusual bronze seed heads.

SITE & SOIL
14

PROPAGATION
9

FLOWER TIME
August — October

TOP TIPS
Easy to grow, but disappointing in prolonged wet weather.

SCABIOSA

S. caucasica 'Clive Greaves'
Border Scabious

Border perennial

A popular border plant which has a long flowering period. The frilly-edged 8 cm wide blooms are attractive but there is never an abundance at any one time.

S. caucasica

VARIETIES

S. caucasica – 60 cm. Lavender.
S. c. 'Clive Greaves' – 60 cm. Lavender.
S. c. 'Miss Willmott' – 90 cm. White.
S. c. 'Compliment' – 60 cm. Blue.
S. c. 'Moerheim Blue' – 60 cm. Violet.
S. c. 'Butterfly Blue' – 30 cm. Blue.
S. lucida – 20 cm. Lavender.

SITE & SOIL
14

PROPAGATION
6

FLOWER TIME
June — October

TOP TIPS
Keep watch for slugs in spring and dead-head faded blooms.

SCAEVOLA

S. aemula 'Blue Fan'
Fairy Fan Flower

Bedding plant: tender perennial

In the 1990s this conservatory plant appeared in the garden centres as a bedding plant. The petals are borne on one side of the flower, giving a fan-like appearance.

S. aemula 'Blue Fan'

VARIETIES

S. aemula – 30 cm. Blue or lilac. 3 cm wide flowers. Thick trailing stems. Dandelion-like leaves. There are a few varieties:
S. a. 'Blue Fan' – White-eyed lilac. The most popular variety.
S. a. 'Blue Wonder' – White-eyed blue.
S. a. 'Alba' – White. Not easy to find.

SITE & SOIL
2

PROPAGATION
11

FLOWER TIME
June — September

TOP TIPS
Stems are stiff so don't expect it to trail vertically in a hanging basket.

SCHIZANTHUS

S. pinnatus 'Bouquet'

Poor Man's Orchid

Bedding plant: half-hardy annual

Each flower looks like a miniature orchid, streaked or spotted in a wide range of colours. The blooms are borne in large numbers above ferny foliage. Pick a sheltered spot.

S. pinnatus 'Hit Parade'

VARIETIES

S. pinnatus – 25-90 cm. Various. 8 cm wide 2-lipped flowers.
S. p. 'Giant Hybrids' – 90 cm. Various. Grow in the greenhouse — for outdoors choose a compact variety. Examples are:
S. p. 'Hit Parade' – 30 cm. Various.
S. p. 'Star Parade' – 25 cm. Various.
S. p. 'Bouquet' – 25 cm. Various.

SITE & SOIL
2

PROPAGATION
7

FLOWER TIME
July — August

TOP TIPS
Good drainage is essential. Pinch out stem tips to induce bushiness.

SCHIZOSTYLIS

S. coccinea 'Mrs. Hegarty'

Kaffir Lily

Border perennial

Despite its common name it is a member of the iris and not the lily family. Rhizomes can be bought for spring planting but it is more usual to buy a pot-grown specimen.

VARIETIES

S. coccinea – 60 cm. Various.
S. c. 'Mrs. Hegarty' – 60 cm. Pink. Early flowering.
S. c. 'Viscountess Byng' – 60 cm. Pink. Late flowering.
S. c. 'Sunrise' – 60 cm. Salmon-pink. Large flowers.
S. c. 'Major' – 80 cm. Dark red. Large flowers.

S. coccinea

SITE & SOIL
9

PROPAGATION
6

FLOWER TIME
September — November

TOP TIPS
Cannot tolerate dryness, so water copiously in dry weather.

SCILLA

S. non-scripta

Bluebell, Squill

Bulb

Bluebells are a familiar sight in spring, but there are other types of Scilla. There are winter-flowering dwarfs for the rockery and summer-flowering cluster-headed ones.

VARIETIES

S. tubergeniana – 8 cm. Dark-striped pale blue. February-March.
S. siberica – 15 cm. Blue. Siberian Squill. March-April.
S. non-scripta – 25 cm. Blue. English Bluebell. April-May.
S. peruviana – 30 cm. Blue or white. Cuban Lily. Rounded clusters of starry flowers. May-June.

S. siberica

SITE & SOIL
3

PROPAGATION
1

FLOWER TIME
Depends on species

TOP TIPS
Bulbs should be planted as soon as possible after purchase.

SEDUM

Ice Plant, Stonecrop

Rockery perennial
Border perennial

S. spectabile

S. kamtschaticum 'Variegatum'

S. spathulifolium

A large group of fleshy-leaved plants which thrive in hot and dry conditions. Some are tall enough to be grown as border plants and are usually called Ice Plants — the flower-heads are large plates of tiny flowers which appear in late summer. The low-growing ones are the Stonecrops which sprawl or form a mat over the ground or over rocks — hence the name. Starry flowers which are usually yellow open in early summer and are borne singly or in flat heads. Most are evergreen and are easy to grow and propagate.

S. 'Autumn Joy'

VARIETIES

S. spectabile – 30-60 cm. Pink or purple. The basic Ice Plant. August-October. Varieties include **'Brilliant'** (Pink), and **'Iceberg'** (White). Hybrids are more popular — look for **S. 'Ruby Glow'** (Red), **S. 'Autumn Joy'** (Reddish-brown) and **S. 'Bertram Anderson'** (Dark pink).
S. telephium 'Munstead Dark Red' – 45 cm. Red. August-September.
S. acre – 5 cm. Yellow. Common Stonecrop. June-July.
S. album 'Coral Carpet' – 10 cm. Pink. Less invasive than S. acre.
S. spurium – 10 cm. Various.
S. kamtschaticum 'Variegatum' – 10 cm. Yellow/orange.
S. spathulifolium – 8 cm. Yellow.

S. acre

FLOWER TIME
Depends on species

TOP TIPS
Dry, infertile soil is no problem, but choose with care if your rockery is small. There are rampant ones to avoid — S. acre can easily become a weed.

SITE & SOIL
2

PROPAGATION
2

SEMPERVIVUM

S. arachnoideum
Houseleek

Rockery perennial

S. tectorum

Thick flower stalks bearing a number of multi-petalled flowers in yellow, red or purple appear in summer and autumn. The leaves are fleshy and grouped into a ball-like rosette.

VARIETIES

S. tectorum – 10 cm. Pink or purple. Common Houseleek.
S. montanum – 8 cm. Pink or purple. Hairy leaves.
Decorative foliage types include:
S. arachnoideum – 8 cm. Pink. Cobwebby white hairs on leaves.
S. 'Commander Hay' – 10 cm. Pink. Green-tipped purple leaves.

FLOWER TIME
July — August

TOP TIPS
The mother rosette will die when flowering is finished.

SITE & SOIL
1

PROPAGATION
33

SIDALCEA

S. 'Rose Queen'

Prairie Mallow

Border perennial

Looks like a small hollyhock but it is neither short-lived nor disease-prone like its taller relative. Each silky saucer-shaped bloom on the flower spikes is 4-5 cm wide.

S. malviflora

VARIETIES

S. malviflora – 80 cm-1.2 m. Pink. The basic species. Hybrids rather than the species are grown:
S. 'Rose Queen' – Rose-pink.
S. 'Party Girl' – Pink.
S. 'Elsie Heugh' – Pink.
S. 'William Smith' – Salmon.
S. 'Croftway Red' – Red.
S. candida – 45 cm. White.

SITE & SOIL
3

PROPAGATION
6

FLOWER TIME
June — August

TOP TIPS
Cut down the stems to ground level after flowering.

SILENE

S. dioica

Campion

Rockery perennial
Border perennial

Most Campions are rockery perennials which spread slowly to form a low carpet. They relish dry starved soil and in summer or autumn produce flat-faced flowers.

S. schafta

VARIETIES

S. acaulis – 5 cm. White or pink. Moss Campion. May-June.
S. uniflora 'Flore Pleno' – 15 cm. White. Double. July-October.
S. schafta – 15 cm. Pink. June-October. Good carpeter.
S. s. 'Abbotswood' – Dark pink.
S. dioica – 75 cm. Pink. Most popular border Campion.

SITE & SOIL
1

PROPAGATION
31

FLOWER TIME
Depends on species

TOP TIPS
Not worth growing if the site is shady or poorly drained.

SILENE

S. coeli-rosa
'Brilliant Mixed'

Catchfly

Hardy annual

The annual varieties of Silene are less popular than the perennial types grown in the rockery. Viscaria is the only one you are likely to find in the seed catalogues.

S. coeli-rosa

VARIETIES

S. coeli-rosa – 30 cm. Various. Viscaria. 3 cm wide flowers recommended for cutting. Mixtures are the usual choice:
S. c. 'Brilliant Mixed' – Various. Single colours are available:
S. c. 'Blue Angel' – Blue.
S. pendula – 15 cm. Pink. Nodding Catchfly. Drooping flowers.

SITE & SOIL
3

PROPAGATION
21

FLOWER TIME
June — August

TOP TIPS
Grow in a massed group rather than as spaced plants.

SISYRINCHIUM

S. striatum
Sisyrinchium

Border perennial
Rockery perennial

S. angustifolium

Like other members of the iris family it produces erect fans of sword-like leaves but the blooms are six-petalled stars or bells. Self-seeds very readily — can be a nuisance.

VARIETIES

S. striatum – 60 cm. Pale yellow. Whorls of flowers — the usual border Sisyrinchium. June-July.
S. s. 'Aunt May' – 60 cm. Pale yellow. Cream-striped leaves. Several rockery dwarfs are available. Various. June-September.
S. brachypus – 15 cm. Yellow.
S. angustifolium – 15 cm. Blue.

SITE & SOIL
9

PROPAGATION
2

FLOWER TIME
Depends on species

TOP TIPS
Fans die after flowering, so lift and divide every 2 years.

SMILACINA

S. racemosa
Smilacina

Border perennial

S. stellata

Arching stems bear clusters of tiny flowers at the tips — the scented starry blooms are often followed by red berries. A woodland plant which is best left undisturbed.

VARIETIES

S. racemosa – 90 cm. Creamy-white. False Spikenard. Grows into large clumps. 15 cm long flower clusters. The only species you are likely to see and the best one to choose.
S. stellata – 60 cm. White. Star-flowered Lily of the Valley. Can be invasive.

SITE & SOIL
20

PROPAGATION
6

FLOWER TIME
May — June

TOP TIPS
Moisture-retentive soil and some shade are essential. Mulch in spring.

SOLIDAGO

S. 'Goldenmosa'
Golden Rod

Border perennial

S. 'Golden Wings'

The heads of tiny yellow flowers in late summer are a welcome feature in the border, but the familiar S. canadensis is a tall and weedy plant. Grow a hybrid instead.

VARIETIES

Hybrids have been bred from **S. canadensis**, **S. virgaurea** etc – 30 cm-1.8 m. Yellow.
S. 'Queenie' – 30 cm.
S. 'Goldenmosa' – 80 cm. Mimosa-like flowers.
S. 'Golden Wings' – 1.8 m.
S. 'Lemore' – 70 cm. Solidago x Aster hybrid.

SITE & SOIL
3

PROPAGATION
2

FLOWER TIME
July — September

TOP TIPS
Mulch in spring, use twigs for support and water in summer.

STACHYS

Stachys

S. byzantina

Border perennial

S. macrantha

The popular Stachys (Lamb's Ears) is a woolly-leaved ground cover grown for its evergreen foliage rather than its spikes of insignificant flowers.

VARIETIES

S. byzantina – 45 cm. Pale purple. Lamb's Ears. 1 cm long flowers on upright spikes. July-August.
S. b. 'Cotton Boll' – 45 cm. White. Bobble-like flowers.
S. macrantha – 60 cm. Pale purple. Big Betony. 4 cm long tubular flowers. All-green deciduous leaves. May-July.

SITE & SOIL
4

PROPAGATION
2

FLOWER TIME
Depends on species

TOP TIPS
Cut off flowering spikes once the blooms have faded.

STOKESIA

Stokes' Aster

S. laevis

Border perennial

S. laevis

An evergreen perennial for the front of the border. The cornflower-like blooms first appear in midsummer and continue to open until the first frosts arrive.

VARIETIES

S. laevis – 30-45 cm. Lilac. The only species you will find. Long, narrow leaves. 8 cm wide saucer-shaped blooms – petals are deeply notched.
S. l. 'Alba' – White.
S. l. 'Blue Star' – Pale blue.
S. l. 'Blue Moon' – Blue.
S. l. 'Superba' – Lavender.

SITE & SOIL
2

PROPAGATION
6

FLOWER TIME
July — October

TOP TIPS
Mulch in spring. Dead-head faded blooms and water during dry spells.

SYMPHYTUM

Comfrey

S. 'Hidcote Pink'

Border perennial

S. ibericum

A tough ground cover which will succeed under a wide range of conditions. Drooping heads of tubular flowers are produced in late spring or early summer.

VARIETIES

S. ibericum – 40 cm. Pale yellow.
S. officinale – 1-1.5 m. Pink, mauve or yellow. Common Comfrey. Rough, hairy leaves.
S. 'Hidcote Pink' – 45 cm. Pink.
S. 'Goldsmith' – 30 cm. Pink, blue or yellow. Yellow-marked leaves.
S. caucasicum – 60 cm. Blue.
S. uplandicum – 1 m. Pale purple.

SITE & SOIL
4

PROPAGATION
6

FLOWER TIME
May — June

TOP TIPS
Take care — some are invasive and all can cause a rash.

TAGETES

Bedding plant: half-hardy annual

T. patula hybrid

T. 'Naughty Marietta'

T. 'Scarlet Sophia'

T. 'Tiger Eyes'

SITE & SOIL

2

PROPAGATION

7

French Marigold

The half-hardy marigolds are a basic feature of summer-flowering beds and containers — they are the most popular source of reds and oranges. They are easy to raise from seed, reliable under all sorts of conditions, long-flowering from early summer until the first frosts arrive and are inexpensive to buy as seedlings for planting out. The favourite marigold is the French Marigold (T. patula hybrids). The varieties bear masses of 5 cm wide single, semi-double or double blooms on 15-30 cm high bushy plants.

VARIETIES

Hybrids of **T. patula** range from white to dark red. The single varieties used to dominate the range:

T. 'Naughty Marietta' – 30 cm. Yellow/maroon. An old favourite.
T. 'Disco' Series – 15 cm. Various.
T. 'Fantasia' Series – 15 cm. Various.
Nowadays doubles are more popular:
T. 'Aurora' Series – 20 cm. Various.
T. 'Sophia' Series – 25 cm. Various.
T. 'Safari' Series – 25 cm. Various.
T. 'Petite Mixed' – 15 cm. Various.
Crested varieties have crowded, tightly-rolled inner petals:
T. 'Tiger Eyes' – 25 cm. Orange/red.
T. 'Honeycomb' – 25 cm. Yellow/ orange.

T. 'Aurora Mixed'

T. 'Honeycomb'

FLOWER TIME
June — October

TOP TIPS
Plant out before the flowers open — avoid plants in full flower. Water when the weather is dry and keep watch for slugs. Dead-head spent blooms to prolong the display.

TAGETES

Bedding plant: half-hardy annual

T. 'Lemon Gem'

SITE & SOIL

2

PROPAGATION

7

T. 'Starfire'

Tagetes

The small-flowered varieties on upright plants are listed as Tagetes or Signet Marigolds. 15-25 cm high ferny-leaved plants bear masses of 1-3 cm wide single flowers.

VARIETIES

The varieties are hybrids of **T. signata** (T. tenuifolia):
T. 'Gem' Series – 15-25 cm. Various. The most popular group — look for **'Lemon Gem'**, **'Golden Gem'**, **'Tangerine Gem'** etc.
T. 'Paprika' – 20 cm. Gold-edged red. Attractive bicolour.
T. 'Starfire' – 25 cm. Various.

FLOWER TIME
June — October

TOP TIPS
For genus description and cultural notes see French Marigold.

TAGETES

T. 'Red Seven Star'
African Marigold

Bedding plant:
half-hardy annual

T. 'Doubloon'

T. 'Nell Gwynn'

SITE & SOIL
2

PROPAGATION
7

African Marigolds are taller, more upright and with fewer but larger flowers than French Marigolds. Between the two are their hybrids — the Afro-French Marigolds.

VARIETIES

African Marigolds have double ball-like flowers:
T. 'Doubloon' – 80 cm. Yellow.
T. 'First Lady' – 50 cm. Yellow.
T. 'Inca Mixed' – 30 cm. Various.
Afro-French Marigolds include:
T. 'Nell Gwynn' – 30 cm. Yellow/red. Single.
T. 'Red Seven Star' – 30 cm. Red.

FLOWER TIME
June — October

TOP TIPS
For genus description and cultural notes see French Marigold.

TANACETUM

T. coccineum 'Brenda'
Pyrethrum, Tansy

Border perennial
Rockery perennial

T. coccineum 'Vanessa'

SITE & SOIL
2

PROPAGATION
6

The border types with large flowers are sold as Pyrethrum — the daisy-like blooms are borne singly on long stems. The species with tiny button-like blooms is Tansy.

VARIETIES

T. coccineum – 45-75 cm. Various. Pyrethrum. May-June.
T. c. 'Brenda' – Dark pink. Single.
T. c. 'James Kelway' – Vermilion. Single.
T. c. 'Vanessa' – Yellow/pink. Double.
T. vulgare – 90 cm. Yellow. Common Tansy. August-October.

FLOWER TIME
Depends on species

TOP TIPS
Provide support for tall varieties. Water during dry weather.

TANACETUM

T. parthenium 'Snow Puffs'
Feverfew

Bedding plant:
half-hardy annual

T. parthenium 'Golden Ball'

SITE & SOIL
2

PROPAGATION
7

Single varieties were once popular but not any more. The compact leafy mounds are covered with masses of cushion-like flowers in late summer.

VARIETIES

T. parthenium (Matricaria eximia) – 10-30 cm. White or yellow. 3 cm wide blooms. The basic species.
T. p. 'White Star' – White/yellow. Single. Difficult to find.
T. p. 'Golden Ball' – Yellow. Ball-like head of tiny flowers.
T. p. 'Snow Puffs' – White. Outer ring of guard petals.

FLOWER TIME
July — September

TOP TIPS
Can be grown as a short-lived perennial. Water in dry weather.

TELLIMA
Fringecup

Border perennial

Like its relative Tiarella this semi-evergreen has veined, lobed leaves. It may look similar but Tellima has bell-shaped flowers and not white frothy stars like Tiarella.

T. grandiflora

VARIETIES

T. grandiflora – 45 cm. Pale green changing to pink. 1 cm wide flowers on upright spikes. Heart- or kidney-shaped leaves with scalloped edges. Good drought resistance.
T. g. 'Purpurea' – Pink-edged pale green. Purplish leaves.
T. g. 'Odorata' – Pale green. Sweet-smelling.

SITE & SOIL
4

PROPAGATION
2

FLOWER TIME
May — June

TOP TIPS
Mulch in spring. Remove faded flowers. Lift and divide every few years.

TEUCRIUM
Germander

T. pyrenaicum

Rockery perennial
Border perennial

The low-growing varieties form leafy mounds and are suitable for the rockery or front of the border. They are evergreen and bear two-lipped flowers throughout the summer.

T. chamaedrys

VARIETIES

T. chamaedrys – 30 cm. Rosy-purple. Wall Germander. Leaves dark green above, grey below.
T. aroanium – 10 cm. Purplish-blue. Silvery-grey leaves.
T. pyrenaicum – 30 cm. Lilac/cream. Trailing stems.
T. subspinosum – 5 cm. Pink. Small flowers. Spiny stems.

SITE & SOIL
1

PROPAGATION
10

FLOWER TIME
June — August

TOP TIPS
Choose carefully — some Germanders are shrubs and not all are hardy.

THALICTRUM
Meadow Rue

T. aquilegiifolium 'Album'

Border perennial
Rockery perennial

The stems are slender and the leaflets have the appearance of Maidenhair Fern. A plant for the back of the border — the tiny flowers are borne in large heads.

T. delavayi

VARIETIES

T. delavayi – 1.5 m. Lavender. 15 cm wide flower-heads. June-September. Popular species.
T. d. 'Hewitt's Double' – 90 cm. Mauve. Double.
T. aquilegiifolium – 90 cm. Various. June-July. Fluffy flowers.
T. a. 'Album' – 90 cm. White.
T. kiusianum – 15 cm. Mauve.

SITE & SOIL
13

PROPAGATION
2

FLOWER TIME
Depends on species

TOP TIPS
Provide support for the stems. Cut down in late autumn.

THUNBERGIA

T. alata 'Susie'

Black-eyed Susan

Bedding plant: half-hardy annual

A few varieties of this conservatory plant can be grown as annuals to climb or trail in the garden. The showy flowers stand out above the arrow-shaped leaves.

T. alata

VARIETIES

T. alata – 1.2-3 m. Cream, yellow, pale brown or orange. 5 cm wide funnel-shaped flowers — the throats are usually dark purple.

T. a. 'Susie' – 1.2 m. White, yellow or orange. The only one you are likely to find.

T. fragrans 'Angel Wings' – Yellow-eyed white.

SITE & SOIL
1

PROPAGATION
7

FLOWER TIME
July — September

TOP TIPS
A sunny spot sheltered from strong winds is essential.

THYMUS

T. citriodorus 'Silver Queen'

Thyme

Rockery perennial
Border perennial

The carpeters form large mats of aromatic leaves and a covering of tiny flowers — the bushy ones are much taller and are planted in the rockery or border.

T. serpyllum

VARIETIES

T. serpyllum – 2-8 cm. Pink. Spread 60 cm. The basic carpeter.

T. s. 'Pink Chintz' – Pink.

T. s. 'Albus' – White.

T. 'Doone Valley' – Lavender.

T. citriodorus – 30 cm. Lavender. The basic bushy Thyme.

T. c. 'Silver Queen' – White-edged leaves.

SITE & SOIL
7

PROPAGATION
2

FLOWER TIME
May — July

TOP TIPS
Soil must not be acid nor heavy. Trim back annually.

TIARELLA

T. wherryi

Foam Flower

Border perennial

Mounds of evergreen leaves which turn bronze or red in winter bear spikes of small frothy flowers in early summer. It will grow quite happily under trees.

T. cordifolia

VARIETIES

T. cordifolia – 20 cm. White. Tiny star-shaped flowers. May-July. Most popular species. The leafy carpet is dense — can be invasive.

T. wherryi – 30 cm. White. Longer flowering — June-September. Non-invasive.

T. polyphylla – 50 cm. White. May-July.

SITE & SOIL
20

PROPAGATION
2

FLOWER TIME
Depends on species

TOP TIPS
Needs some shade — will do badly in full sun or if kept short of water.

TITHONIA

T. rotundifolia
'Yellow Torch'

Mexican Sunflower

Bedding plant:
half-hardy annual

A bold annual for the middle of the bed or the back of the border. The popular one grows about 75 cm high, but there are 1.5 m giants to cover large and unsightly areas.

VARIETIES

T. rotundifolia 'Goldfinger'

T. rotundifolia – 1.5 m. Orange-red, yellow below. 8 cm wide flowers with central yellow disc. This is the basic species with several varieties:

SITE & SOIL
1

PROPAGATION
19

T. r. 'Torch' – 1.2 m. Orange-red.
T. r. 'Yellow Torch' – 1.2 m. Yellow.
T. r. 'Goldfinger' – 75 cm. Orange. The most popular and compact variety.

FLOWER TIME
July — September

TOP TIPS
Protect young growth from slugs. Tall varieties require staking.

TORENIA

T. fournieri
'Susie Wong'

Wishbone Flower

Bedding plant:
half-hardy annual

Despite its exotic appearance this weak-stemmed annual is quite easy to raise from seed and will flower abundantly in sun or partial shade. Provide support or leave to trail.

VARIETIES

T. fournieri
'Pink Panda'

T. fournieri – 30 cm. Pale violet. 3 cm wide tubular flowers have a yellow-blotched purple lower lip.

SITE & SOIL
4

PROPAGATION
7

T. f. 'Clown Mixed' – 20 cm. Various. Velvety flowers.
T. f. 'Pink Panda' – 15 cm. White/pink.
T. f. 'Susie Wong' – 20 cm. Chocolate-eyed yellow.

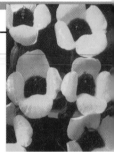

FLOWER TIME
July — September

TOP TIPS
Pinch out stem tips of seedlings to grow as a bushy plant.

TRADESCANTIA

T. andersoniana
'Isis'

Spiderwort

Border perennial

Three-petalled flowers appear from early summer to early autumn, although each bloom lasts for only a day. A grow-anywhere plant, in sun or shade and in wet or dry soil.

VARIETIES

T. andersoniana

T. andersoniana (T. virginiana) – 45-60 cm. Purple. 3 cm wide flowers. 30 cm long sword-shaped leaves.

SITE & SOIL
10

PROPAGATION
2

T. a. 'Osprey' – White.
T. a. 'Isis' – Violet-blue.
T. a. 'Purewell Giant' – Red.
T. a. 'Pauline' – Lilac.
T. a. 'Innocence' – White.

FLOWER TIME
June — September

TOP TIPS
Support the stems if necessary. Cut back in late autumn.

TROLLIUS

T. chinensis 'Golden Queen'

Globe Flower

Bog plant
Border perennial

T. 'Orange Princess'

Adequate moisture is essential — this is a plant for the bog garden or a humus-rich border. In early summer large buttercup-like flowers are borne on erect stems.

VARIETIES

T. cultorum – 50-75 cm. Yellow or orange. 3-6 cm wide flowers. Numerous hybrids but not the species are available:

SITE & SOIL

16

T. 'Alabaster' – Pale cream.

PROPAGATION

2

T. 'Lemon Queen' – Yellow.
T. 'Orange Princess' – Orange.
T. chinensis 'Golden Queen' – 90 cm. Pale orange. Large flowers.

FLOWER TIME
May — June

TOP TIPS
Mulch in spring — water in dry weather. Cut down in autumn.

TROPAEOLUM

T. 'Alaska Mixed'

Nasturtium

Bedding plant:
hardy annual

The familiar nasturtium with its spurred flowers has many uses in the garden — there are climbers for walls, semi-trailers for window boxes and bushy dwarfs for bedding.

VARIETIES

Many hybrids of **T. majus** are available:

T. 'Tom Thumb Red'

SITE & SOIL

2

T. 'Tall Mixed' – 2 m. Various.
T. 'Gleam' Series – 30 cm. Various.

PROPAGATION

9

T. 'Whirlybird' – 30 cm. Various.
T. 'Alaska' – 20 cm. Various.
T. 'Tom Thumb' – 15 cm. Various.
T. peregrinum – 3 m. Yellow. Canary Creeper. Lobed leaves.

FLOWER TIME
June

TOP TIPS
Best sown where they are to grow. Watch for blackfly.

TROPAEOLUM

T. polyphyllum

Perennial Nasturtium

Hardy perennial
Bulb

The perennial varieties grow from rhizomes or tubers and are much less popular than the annual ones. These climbers or trailers are not as easy to grow.

VARIETIES

T. speciosum – 3 m. Red. Flame Nasturtium. Hardy climber. July-September.

T. tuberosum 'Ken Aslet'

SITE & SOIL

18

T. tuberosum 'Ken Aslet' – 3 m. Orange-backed yellow. Tender climber — lift and store tubers over winter. September.

PROPAGATION

1

T. polyphyllum – 1 m. Yellow. Hardy trailer. June-July.

FLOWER TIME
Depends on species

TOP TIPS
T. speciosum needs humus-rich soil and shade at the roots.

TULIPA

Bulb

T. 'Keizerskroon'

T. 'Monte Carlo'

Early Tulip

Tulips are divided into 15 Divisions in the textbooks. To make things easier Tulips have been put into five groups in this book — the first four (Early, Late, Large-flowered and Fancy) are the Garden Tulips which are generally lifted every year and the final group contains the Botanical Tulips which are left in the ground over winter. Described here are the Early varieties — like all Garden Tulips plant 15-20 cm deep in November-December and lift when the foliage turns yellow. Store bulbs in a frost-free place.

VARIETIES

Single Early Tulips are cup-shaped – smaller than Double Earlies. 20-25 cm. Strong stems — blooms open flat.

T. **'Apricot Beauty'** – Orange-tinged salmon.
T. **'Bellona'** – Yellow. Fragrant.
T. **'Keizerskroon'** – Yellow/red.
T. **'Diana'** – White.
T. **'General de Wet'** – Orange.

Double Early Tulips are long-lasting – good for cutting. 25-45 cm. Strong stems, but may bend over after heavy rain.

T. **'Peach Blossom'** – Dark pink.
T. **'Orange Nassau'** – Red-flushed orange.
T. **'Electra'** – Red.
T. **'Monte Carlo'** – Yellow.

T. 'Bellona'

T. 'Electra'

FLOWER TIME

Mid April

TOP TIPS

Garden Tulips can be left undisturbed for 3 years if planted at recommended depth and soil is not acid. Remove flowers and foliage when they start to fade.

TULIPA

Bulb

T. 'Golden Harvest'

T. 'Bonanza'

Late Tulip

Late Tulips have large flowers and bloom about one month after the Earlies. Single Lates are tall — Double Lates are shorter and are less popular than Double Earlies.

VARIETIES

Single Late Tulips are square or oval. 60-75 cm.

T. **'Clara Butt'** – Salmon.
T. **'Golden Harvest'** – Yellow.
T. **'Maureen'** – White.

Double Late Tulips are cup-shaped. 45-60 cm.

T. **'Bonanza'** – Yellow/red.
T. **'Mount Tacoma'** – White.

FLOWER TIME

Mid May

TOP TIPS

For planting notes and top tips see Early Tulip above.

TULIPA

Bulb

T. 'Garden Party'

T. 'Apeldoorn Elite'

Large-flowered Tulip

These varieties bloom between the Early and Late Tulips. Darwin Hybrids are very large on tall stems — Triumph Tulips have smaller flowers on shorter stems.

VARIETIES

Darwin Hybrids are usually rounded. 60 cm.
T. 'Apeldoorn' Series – Various.
T. 'Elizabeth Arden' – Dark pink.
Triumph Tulips are conical then rounded. 45 cm.
T. 'Garden Party' – Red-edged white.
T. 'Cassini' – Red.

FLOWER TIME
Late April — early May

TOP TIPS
For planting notes see Early Tulip section on page 108.

TULIPA

Bulb

T. 'Bellflower'

T. 'Texas Flame'

Fancy-flowered Tulip

Lily-flowered Tulips have long pointed petals, Fringed Tulips have finely-fringed petals, Viridiflora Tulips are partly green and Parrot Tulips have frilled petals.

VARIETIES

T. 'West Point' – 50 cm. Yellow. Lily-flowered Tulip. Strong stems.
T. 'Bellflower' – 50 cm. Pink. Fringed Tulip.
T. 'Greenland' – 35 cm. Rose-edged green. Viridiflora Tulip.
T. 'Texas Flame' – 50 cm. Red/yellow. Parrot Tulip. Stems may need support.

FLOWER TIME
Mid May

TOP TIPS
For planting notes see Early Tulip section on page 108.

TULIPA

Bulb

T. biflora

*T. greigii
'Red Riding Hood'*

Botanical Tulip

Here you will find species and their varieties together with hybrids of known species. There is a wide range of flower shapes, stem heights and times of flowering.

VARIETIES

T. kaufmanniana hybrids – 15-25 cm. Various. March.
T. fosteriana hybrids – 30-50 cm. Various. April.
T. greigii hybrids – 20-35 cm. Various. April-May.
T. biflora – 15 cm. Yellow/white. 5 blooms per stem. March.
T. praestans – 15 cm. Red. April.

FLOWER TIME
Depends on species

TOP TIPS
Plant bulbs 10 cm deep and leave in the ground to spread.

UVULARIA

U. grandiflora

Merrybells

Border perennial

A shade-lover with upright stems and clasping leaves. In spring the branching stems bear pendent bells with narrow and twisted petals. Grow it under trees.

VARIETIES

U. grandiflora – 75 cm. Yellow. Large Merrybells. 5 cm long tubular flowers which hang down on slender stalks. April-May.
U. g. 'Pallida' – Pale yellow.
U. perfoliata – 60 cm. Pale yellow. 3 cm long flowers. May-June.
U. sessilifolia – 60 cm. Cream. May-June.

U. grandiflora

SITE & SOIL
8

PROPAGATION
3

FLOWER TIME
Depends on species

TOP TIPS
The situation must be right — moist, acid and shady.

VERBASCUM

V. bombyciferum

Mullein

Border perennial
Rockery perennial

The tall varieties with spikes of showy saucer-shaped blooms above a rosette of woolly leaves are the most popular ones, but there are a few dwarfs for the rockery.

VARIETIES

V. olympicum – 2 m. Yellow. 3 cm wide flowers. Short-lived.
V. bombyciferum – 2 m. Yellow.
V. chiaxii – 1 m. Various.
V. c. 'Pink Domino' – Pink.
V. c. 'Gainsborough' – Pale yellow.
V. 'Helen Johnson' – 1 m. Copper.
V. phoeniceum – 1 m. Purple.
V. 'Letitia' – 30 cm. Yellow.

V. phoeniceum

SITE & SOIL
1

PROPAGATION
6

FLOWER TIME
June — August

TOP TIPS
Avoid rich soil. Stake tall varieties. Cut down in autumn.

VERBENA

V. 'Tapien Pink'

Verbena

Bedding plant:
half-hardy annual

Small flowers, usually fragrant and white-eyed, are borne in clusters. The upright types have long been used for bedding and trailing ones are now popular.

VARIETIES

Many named hybrids are available:
V. 'Novalis Mixed' – 20 cm. Various. Upright. Popular.
V. 'Romance Mixed' – 15 cm. Various. Spreading.
V. 'Imagination' – 30 cm. Violet-blue. Spreading.
V. 'Tapien' Series – 60 cm. Various. Trailing. Popular.

V. 'Novalis Red'

SITE & SOIL
2

PROPAGATION
7/11

FLOWER TIME
July — October

TOP TIPS
Raising from seed is not easy — use plugs or take cuttings.

VERONICA

Speedwell

Border perennial
Rockery perennial

V. spicata

V. prostrata

The garden speedwells have a remarkable range of heights — there are alpine varieties which grow to less than 10 cm high and there are back of the border plants which reach 1.5 m. The small flat-faced white, blue, purple or pink flowers are usually borne on narrow spikes — these should be cut down once the blooms have faded. Generally trouble-free, but winter waterlogging will kill them and some of the mat-forming rockery types can be invasive. They will grow in a wide range of soils, including chalky ones.

V. gentianoides

V. cinerea

VARIETIES

V. (Veronicastrum) virginicum 'Album' – 1.5 m. White. Culver's Root. July-September.

V. exaltata – 1.2 m. Pale blue. August-September.

V. longifolia – 1.2 m. Lilac. August.

V. gentianoides – 45 cm. Pale blue. Early flowering — May-June.

V. incana – 45 cm. Blue. Silvery semi-evergreen leaves. June-July.

V. i. 'Wendy' – 45 cm. Blue.

V. spicata – 45 cm. Blue.

V. teucrium 'Shirley Blue' – 25 cm. Bright blue.

V. peduncularis – 15 cm. Blue. Bronzy leaves.

V. prostrata – 8-10 cm. Lilac.

V. cinerea – 10 cm. Lilac.

FLOWER TIME

Depends on species

TOP TIPS

Mulch in spring and water when the weather is dry. Tall-growing varieties will need some support when in flower. Humus-rich soil is preferred, but it must be free-draining.

VIOLA

V. 'Universal Mixed'

Pansy

Bedding plant: hardy annual
Bedding plant: hardy biennial

V. 'Rippling Waters'

Low-growing familiar flat-faced flowers — short-lived perennial usually grown as an annual or biennial. Dividing line between Pansies and Violas is not clear-cut — see page 112.

VARIETIES

Many hybrids – 15-25 cm. Various. Winter (November-May) varieties are grown as biennials — dominant series is **V. 'Universal'**. Summer (June-October) varieties are grown as annuals – **V. 'Swiss Giants'** (Various), **V. 'Rippling Waters'** (White/purple), **V. 'Jolly Joker'** (Orange/purple).

FLOWER TIME

Depends on sowing time

TOP TIPS

Dead-head regularly, protect from slugs and water in dry weather.

VIOLA

V. 'Blue Heaven'

Viola

- Bedding plant: hardy annual
- Bedding plant: hardy biennial

V. 'Johnny Jump-up'

SITE & SOIL
3

PROPAGATION
8

Compared to pansies, varieties listed as violas are generally longer living, more compact, not as easy to grow and with flowers which are smaller (3-5 cm).

VARIETIES

Grow as annuals for June-October flowers or as biennials for March-July flowers.

V. 'Johnny Jump-up' – Mauve/purple/yellow. Old favourite.
V. 'Bambini' – Various. Cat-like face.
V. 'Chantreyland' – Apricot.
V. 'Blue Heaven' – Blue.
V. 'Princess' Series – Various.

FLOWER TIME
Depends on sowing time

TOP TIPS
Dead-head regularly, protect from slugs and water in dry weather.

VIOLA

V. odorata

Violet

- Border perennial
- Rockery perennial

V. cornuta

SITE & SOIL
5

PROPAGATION
1

These Viola species are perennials — some shade is necessary. Do not expect the large and colourful blooms associated with the pansies and violas shown earlier.

VARIETIES

V. odorata – 10-15 cm. White or blue. Sweet Violet. Scented — 2 cm wide. February-April.
V. cornuta – 20 cm. Lilac. Horned Violet. May-August.
V. labradorica 'Purpurea' – 10 cm. Violet-blue. April-June.
V. lutea – 10 cm. Yellow. May-June.
V. biflora – 10 cm. Yellow. May-July.

FLOWER TIME
Depends on species

TOP TIPS
Dead-head regularly, protect from slugs and water in dry weather.

WALDSTEINIA

W. ternata

Waldsteinia

- Border perennial
- Rockery perennial

W. ternata

SITE & SOIL
5

PROPAGATION
1

A plant for shady areas. Surface-rooting stems produce masses of lobed leaves which are studded with clusters of yellow flowers in spring and early summer.

VARIETIES

W. ternata – 10 cm. Yellow. 1 cm wide flowers. Spread 60 cm. The only species you are likely to find. Easy to grow in woodland, front of the border or rockery — semi-evergreen.
W. geoides – 10 cm. Yellow. Flowers larger than W. ternata — leaves are 5-lobed.

FLOWER TIME
April — June

TOP TIPS
It can be invasive so plant it well away from small and delicate plants.

XERANTHEMUM

Common Immortelle

Hardy annual

An annual grown for its 'everlasting' flowers — daisy-like blooms with strawy petals which keep their colour after drying. Tie in bunches and hang upside down.

X. annuum

VARIETIES

X. annuum – 60 cm. Various. Sold as a mixture of single, semi-double and double varieties — 5 cm wide blooms. Silvery leaves.

X. 'Lumina Mixed' – 60 cm. Various. Bushy plants — more attractive than X. annuum for border display.

X. 'Lilac Stars' – 60 cm. Mauve. Silvery-green leaves.

SITE & SOIL
1

PROPAGATION
21

FLOWER TIME
July — September

TOP TIPS
Cut just before the flowers open — remove the leaves.

ZANTEDESCHIA

Z. aethiopica 'Crowborough'
Arum Lily

Bog plant
• Border perennial

Several eye-catching species of Arum or Calla Lily appear in the catalogues but only one is hardy enough to survive outdoors over winter. Moist or wet ground is essential.

Z. aethiopica

VARIETIES

Z. aethiopica – 90 cm. White. 15-25 cm long flowers — grow in boggy ground around a pond or in a moist border. Long arrow-shaped leaves. Never let the soil dry out.

Z. a. 'Crowborough' – White. The hardiest variety.

Z. a. 'Green Goddess' – Cream-centred green. Large flowers.

SITE & SOIL
19

PROPAGATION
1

FLOWER TIME
April — June

TOP TIPS
Choose 'Crowborough' — apply a thick winter mulch to protect the crowns.

ZINNIA

Z. haageana 'Persian Carpet'
Zinnia

Bedding plant: half-hardy annual

Few annuals look as appealing in the seed catalogue, but you will need fertile soil and a warm, dry summer to get similar results. No need to stake.

Z. elegans 'Dahlia-flowered Mixed'

VARIETIES

Named types are varieties of **Z. elegans** or **Z. haageana**.

Z. e. 'Dahlia-flowered Mixed' – 75 cm. Various. 12 cm wide flowers.

Z. e. 'Ruffles' – 60 cm. Various. Pompon-like flower-heads.

Z. e. 'Envy' – 75 cm. Green.

Z. h. 'Persian Carpet' – 40 cm. Various bicolours.

SITE & SOIL
1

PROPAGATION
19

FLOWER TIME
July — October

TOP TIPS
Grow something less fussy if the soil is poor and the site is shady.

CHAPTER 3

BUYING PLANTS

POT-GROWN PLANTS

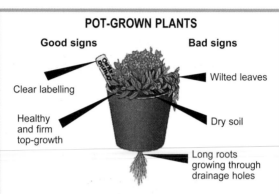

Good signs

Clear labelling

Healthy and firm top-growth

Bad signs

Wilted leaves

Dry soil

Long roots growing through drainage holes

The usual way to buy border and rockery perennials. The pots are most likely to be made of plastic these days. You can plant at any time of the year if the soil is neither frosty nor waterlogged. Tease out matted roots from the surface of the soil ball before planting — water regularly in dry weather after planting. An expensive but the most satisfactory way to buy bedding plants in flower.

PRE-PACKAGED PLANTS

Good sign

Plant completely dormant

Bad signs

Leaf buds beginning to open

Shrivelled or diseased stems

Small white roots growing into the damp packing material

The standard planting material sold by supermarkets and department stores. The bare-rooted perennial has moist peat or moss around the roots and the whole plant is housed inside a labelled polythene bag. Cheaper than the pot-grown counterpart, but you can't always see what you are buying and premature growth may begin in the shop. Planting time is the dormant season between autumn and spring.

STRIPS

A popular way to buy bedding plants for transplanting into beds or containers. The plants are grown in a series of snap-off strips made of rigid white polystyrene or flimsy polyethylene. Each one contains 3 large plants such as geraniums to 10-12 ordinary annuals such as antirrhinums. Roots may be damaged as you prise the plants apart, but this is less likely than with ones grown in undivided trays.

PLUGS

Plugs are larger and more advanced than seedlings — they are small but well-rooted plants which are raised in packs of small cells by the grower. A great advantage is that there is no root disturbance when you pot on the plug into 7.5 cm pots. Plugs can be planted directly into hanging baskets but do not put out baskets with half-hardy annuals if frosty weather is still likely. Trade names include 'Speedplugs', 'Easiplants', 'Starter Plants' and 'Plantlets'.

PACKS & CELLULAR TRAYS

Packs of 4-24 pots made of flimsy plastic and cellular trays of 4-6 cells made of rigid polystyrene have become the standard ways of buying bedding plants. They are more expensive than strips but cheaper than pots with which they share the advantage of avoiding root disturbance at planting time. Avoid packs with lanky stems, abnormally early flowers, discoloured leaves or with roots growing through the bottom of the pack or tray. Do not buy half-hardy annuals until the danger of frost has passed.

SEEDS

Raising annuals and biennials from seed offers two advantages compared with buying seedlings or young plants — it is less expensive and the choice of varieties is much wider. Look for types marked F_1 hybrid — this means that the variety has been carefully bred to have more uniformity and more vigour than the standard types. Some perennials can also be raised in this way, but with many seeds both time and some skill are necessary.

SEEDLINGS

This is the smallest stage at which you can buy plants for growing on, and this is the least expensive way if you have a large area to fill. The seedlings are despatched in a rigid polystyrene pack — 100 is the usual count but some seed houses offer 250 and 400 seedling packs. The tiny plants are at the expanded leaf stage and need to be pricked out shortly after arrival into ordinary or cellular trays filled with compost.

BULBS

Good signs

Bad signs

Firm neck

Stem growth clearly present

Tunic entire — but gaps in tulip skin acceptable

Tunic missing — tissue below damaged

Firm base

Root growth clearly active

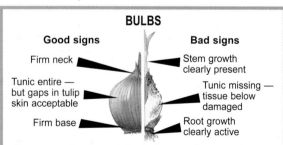

Always examine loose bulbs before you buy — reject any which have clearly come from another box. Look for the good and bad signs — a poor quality bulb will never produce a good quality plant. Large-sized bulbs are usually the best choice, but hyacinths for outdoors should be the medium and not the large grade. The outer scales of lily bulbs should be firm and succulent.

CHAPTER 4

PLANTING

The time to plant depends on the recommended planting season for the specimen and the type of planting material you have bought. With hardy perennials there may be few restrictions but with bulbs and bedding plants the time for planting is much more limited. Choose a day when the soil is in the right condition. Squeeze a handful — it should be wet enough to form a ball but dry enough to shatter when dropped on a hard surface.

With small plants the hole is usually filled with the soil which has been removed. With large plants it is better to use a planting mixture of 1 part topsoil, 1 part moist peat and 3 handfuls of Bone Meal per barrowload.

SMALL DUG-UP PLANTS
•
BEDDING PLANTS

① Dig the hole to fit the roots. The hole should be much wider than it is deep — the roots at the base and at the sides should never have to be bent to fit into the hole. Use the right tool — a trowel is generally the best thing to use

② Plant at the right depth. Set all bedding plants, seedlings and rooted cuttings so that the top of the soil ball is just below ground level. With lifted mature plants use the old soil mark on the stem as your guide

③ Plant properly. For small plants, fill around the soil ball with loose soil and firm with the fingers or the trowel handle. With larger plants, fine soil should be added, each layer being gently compressed with the fists until the hole is full. Handle non-woody plants by the soil ball or the leaves — never by the stem. Water in after planting

BULBS

As a general rule plant as soon as possible after purchase

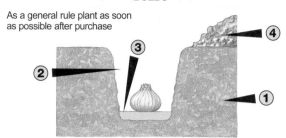

(1) Free drainage is important — dig in coarse sand or grit if the soil is heavy

(2) The width of the hole should be about twice the diameter of the bulb. The depth depends on the type of bulb — as a general rule cover with twice their own height for large bulbs and about their own height for small bulbs

(3) The bottom should be flat — add a layer of grit or peat if the soil is heavy. Push in the bulb and twist gently

(4) Put the earth back and press down gently. Rake over the surface and water in if the weather is dry

---

PRE-PACKAGED BARE-ROOTED PLANTS
•
DUG-UP PLANTS WITH LARGE ROOTS BEYOND THE SOIL BALL

Plant between autumn and spring

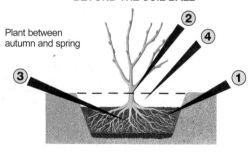

(1) The hole should be wide enough to allow the roots to be spread evenly. Put in a layer of planting mixture (see page 117)

(2) The old soil mark should be level with the surface

(3) Work 2 trowelfuls of planting mixture around the roots. Shake the plant gently up and down — add a little more planting mixture. Firm around the roots with your fists

(4) Fill the hole and firm down with your fists or by gentle treading. Loosen the surface and water in

POT-GROWN PLANTS
•
DUG-UP PLANTS WITH COMPACT SOIL BALL

Planting can take place at any time of the year, but the soil must be neither frozen nor water-logged

(1) The hole should be deep enough to ensure that the top of the soil ball will be below the soil surface after planting — for large plants this space should be about 3 cm. The hole should be wide enough for the soil to be surrounded by a layer of the planting mixture (see page 117). Put a 3 cm layer of this mixture at the bottom of the hole

(2) Water the pot thoroughly at least an hour before planting. Remove the plant very carefully — do not disturb the soil ball. With a pot-grown plant place your hand over the soil and turn the pot over. Gently remove — tap the sides with a trowel if necessary

(3) Examine the exposed surface — cut away circling or tangled roots but do not break up the soil ball. Fill the space between the soil ball and the sides of the hole with planting mixture. Firm down with your hands

(4) After planting there should be a shallow water-holding basin. Water in

CHAPTER 5

PLANT CARE

WATERING

(1) DON'T WAIT Begin before the plants have started to wilt. The time to start watering is when the soil is dry to a depth of 5 cm or more and the foliage is dull. When this occurs depends on the weather and the soil type. A sandy soil dries out much more rapidly than a heavy one, and low humus soil holds less water than organic-rich ground

(2) WATER THOROUGHLY Once you decide to water then do the job thoroughly. Applying a small amount every few days may well do more harm than good as it encourages surface rooting and weed seed germination

(3) USE THE RIGHT TECHNIQUE Decide which method to use. **Point watering** is the simpler method — this calls for holding the spout of a watering can close to the base of each plant and then adding water gently to soak the ground around the root zone. Small beds and containers can be tackled in this way, but it is extremely time consuming if the area to be covered is extensive as you may need to apply 11-18 litres per sq. m. For large beds and borders the obvious choice is **Overall watering**. This involves applying water to the whole area rather than treating each plant. The usual procedure is to walk slowly along the border or around the bed with a hand-held hose and a suitable nozzle. This is a boring job and a common error is to move too quickly so that the plants receive too little water. A sprinkler which can be moved along the border at regular intervals is usually more satisfactory — always carry out this task in the evening and not in hot sunshine. Trickle irrigation through a perforated hose laid close to the plants is perhaps the best method of watering

(4) REPEAT IF NECESSARY Water again if rain does not fall but do not try to keep the land constantly soaked. There must be a period of drying-out between waterings. As a general rule you will need to water every seven days if rain does not fall. The precise interval depends on many factors — to check if water is needed the best plan is to examine the soil 5 cm below the surface. Water immediately if it is dry

HIGH-RISK PLANTS

- All bedding plants for at least 6 weeks after planting

- All perennials for at least 1 season after planting

- All plants in containers

WEEDING

① TRY TO PREVENT WEEDS FROM APPEARING The basic reason why you have a weed problem is bare ground. You can hoe or hand pull the weeds around growing plants and in some cases they can be safely sprayed, but if the soil is uncovered then the problem will return as weed seeds on or near the surface and pieces of perennial weeds start to grow. Digging is often an ineffectual way of controlling weeds on a long term basis. The annual types on the surface are buried, but a host of seeds are brought to the surface. With care some perennial weed roots and bulbs can be removed, but all too often the roots of dandelions, thistles etc and the bulbs of ground elder are spread around. The real answer is to try to cover the surface around plants in beds and borders. You can use a non-living cover (a mulch or weed-proof blanket) or a living one (ground-cover plants). Use one of the following techniques:

Apply a non-living cover One of the purposes of a humus mulch (see page 122) is to suppress weed germination and to make it easier to hand pull ones which may appear. This reduces but does not eliminate the problem. Plastic sheeting provides a complete answer — cover with bark.

Plant ground cover Creeping evergreens with leafy stems provide an excellent way of suppressing weed growth around clumps of perennials. With bedding plants you can solve the ground cover problem by planting them closer together than the usually recommended distance.

② GET RID OF WEEDS PROMPTLY WHEN THEY APPEAR Weeds will appear around your plants in beds or borders unless you have put some form of weed-proof blanket such as plastic sheeting around them. These weeds should be kept in check while they are still small. Use one or more of the methods listed below:

Pull by hand The simplest method for the removal of well-established but easily-uprooted annual weeds in beds and borders and the removal of all types of weeds in the rockery. Use a small fork to uproot perennial weeds — don't pull up by the stems.

Use a hoe The hoe is the traditional enemy of the emerged weed and still remains the most popular control method around growing plants. It will kill large numbers of annual weeds if the surface is dry, the blade is sharp and the cut is kept shallow. Hoeing at regular intervals is needed to starve out the roots of perennial weeds.

Use a weedkiller Numerous contact and translocated weedkillers are available for use around growing plants. Make sure you use the right type — check the label.

FEEDING

Most growing plants will benefit from feeding — with border perennials sprinkle a nitrogen/phosphate/potash fertilizer such as Growmore around the stems. Large and leafy plants such as Dahlias and Florist Chrysanthemums need feeding with a liquid fertilizer at regular intervals to ensure an eye-catching show, and most bulbs also respond to liquid fertilizer as the below-ground storage organs have to be built up for next year's display. Some but not all bedding plants benefit from in-season feeding — annuals do not need to be fed to the same extent as perennials because they do not have to build up a storage root system to tide them over the winter. Rockery perennials need little or no in-season feeding — once a year with a potash-rich feed is ample.

A few rules. The soil should be moist before feeding — water first if the soil is dry. Use no more than the recommended amount and keep solid fertilizers off leaves and flowers.

FERTILIZER TYPES

Soluble or **Liquid fertilizer:** The most popular feeding method — not long lasting

Powder or **Granular fertilizer:** Last longer than liquid ones but take longer to act

Steady-release fertilizer: Coated fertilizer which slowly dissolves — lasts up to 6 months

MULCHING

A mulch is a layer of bulky organic matter which is placed on the soil around the stems. It is generally not applied to bedding plants, but it provides a number of benefits around border perennials.

The soil is kept moist and cool in summer and in winter it is kept warmer than uncovered ground. The addition of humus improves the soil structure and increases worm activity. The growth of annual weeds is suppressed and some mulches provide a small amount of plant food.

The standard time for mulching is May when the soil is warm and moist. Remove surface debris before you begin and get rid of annual weeds by pulling or hoeing. Dig out perennial weeds. Spread a 5-8 cm layer of the mulching material around the stems — leave a small bare space between the mulch and the base of the plant. This mulch can be forked in when autumn arrives, but it is more usual to leave it in place and then top up as necessary in May.

MULCHING MATERIALS

Peat: Widely available, but blows about when dry

Bark: A better choice than peat — lasts for 2-3 years

Well-rotted manure: Inexpensive — the best soil improver

Garden compost: Free — renew annually

HARDENING OFF

Bedding plants raised under glass have tender tissues. Suddenly moving them outdoors in spring exposes them to cold nights and drying winds — the result is a severe check or even death. Hardening off avoids this problem — ventilation is increased during the day and then the plants are moved to a cold frame. After a week or two the lights are raised. Finally they are removed for about a week before planting out.

CUTTING BACK

Some bedding plants have a straggly growth habit and cutting back the stem ends will encourage shoots and flowers. It is also necessary when vigorous plants threaten delicate varieties. Some spring-flowering rockery plants require cutting back in summer to ensure a compact shape next season.

WINTER CARE

Most border perennials, rockery perennials and bulbs have nothing to fear — snow and frost will do them no harm provided the soil does not become waterlogged. Late autumn is the usual time for cutting down dead stems of border perennials. If they are not fully hardy it is wise to put a blanket of straw, bracken, leaf mould or peat over the crowns. Delicate but hardy alpines need protection from winter rains rather than frosts. The standard technique is to cover the plants with a pane of glass supported by bricks.

STAKING

Weak-stemmed plants, tall varieties on exposed sites, large-headed flowers and climbers all need some form of support. It is important to make sure that the display is not spoilt by ugly staking, and as a general rule the stakes should be inserted when the plant is quite small so that the stems can cover them. Use brushwood when you can — twiggy branches pushed into the soil when the stems are about 15 cm high.

This will not do for tall plants — these often require staking with stout canes at planting time. This single-pole technique is suitable for plants with a main stem but should be avoided with bushy plants as an ugly 'drumstick' effect can be produced. Support these plants with three or four canes inserted around the stems — enclose with twine tied around the canes at 15-20 cm intervals.

Use netting, trellis etc for climbers rather than a single stake. Do not tie too tightly and when attaching a climber spread the stems at an angle to form a fan.

PLANT INDEX

125

Acknowledgements

The author wishes to acknowledge the painstaking work of
Gill Jackson and Angelina Gibbs. Grateful acknowledgement is
also made for the help received from Joan Hessayon, Colin Bailey,
Ella Norris, Brian O'Shea, Eric Steele (Colegrave Seeds),
David Arnold (Suttons Seeds), David Kerley (Unwins Seeds) and
Barry Highland (Spot On Digital Imaging Ltd). The author is also
grateful for the photographs and/or artworks received from
Harry Smith Horticultural Photographic Collection, Pat Brindley,
John Dye, Lamontagne/GPL and Howard Rice/GPL.

The Experts —
the world's best-selling gardening books

The Bedding Plant Expert
The Bulb Expert
The Container Expert
The Easy-care Gardening Expert
The Evergreen Expert
The Flower Arranging Expert
The Flower Expert
The Flowering Shrub Expert
The Fruit Expert
The Garden Expert
The Garden DIY Expert
The Greenhouse Expert
The House Plant Expert
The Lawn Expert
The Rock & Water Garden Expert
The Rose Expert
The Tree & Shrub Expert
The Vegetable & Herb Expert